The Camargue

Portrait of a Wilderness

Also by Edwin Mullins

Avignon of the Popes
In Search of Cluny
The Pilgrimage to Santiago

THE CAMARGUE

Portrait of a Wilderness

EDWIN MULLINS

Signal Books
Oxford

First published in 2009 by
Signal Books Limited
36 Minster Road
Oxford
OX4 1LY
www.signalbooks.co.uk

A catalogue record for this book is available from the British Library.

ISBN 978-1-904955-57-3 Paper

Production: Devdan Sen
Cover Design: Baseline Arts
Cover Images: © Jaubert Bernard/Alamy; istockphoto.com
Illustrations: Nicki Averill
Printed in India

Contents

❧

For Ellie, Felix, Tegan, Zöe and Freddie,
my much-loved grandchildren

Author's Preface

I have wanted this book to be a portrait from many angles. The Camargue has always been different things to different people—poets, painters, bird-watchers, farmers, industrialists, crusaders, pilgrims, gypsies, monks, ecologists, cowboys, dreamers, sun-lovers, lovers of folklore, lovers of solitude—and of course tourists, who flock here in their thousands to savour some or all of this rich multiplicity of interests which the place has to offer.

I first set eyes on the Camargue as a student, camping under the stars in the company of merciless mosquitoes, then waking to the magic of flamingos and white egrets flying overhead. Since then I have returned whenever I could, observing the many changes that have taken place over the decades, for better and for worse. Sometimes I applaud. Sometimes I wince, because the Camargue may be a haven for wildlife, but it is also man's playground, and reconciling the two is a balancing-act requiring skill, diplomacy and a strong dose of optimism.

None the less the mystique of the Camargue never fades. At its best it can be a corner of paradise, and at such moments it would take a heart of stone to resist the seductiveness of the place. Let me offer a few snapshots.

At first light a herd of white horses moves as silently as ghosts through the tall reedbeds, only their heads showing, then out into the shallows of the lagoon, their manes sweeping the surface of the water as they drink, the breath from their nostrils merging with the dawn mist as they raise their heads. Then they prance away across the water, their hooves throwing up pearls of spray.

In a field beyond the lagoon the first rays of sunlight pick out a line of black bulls standing motionless and watchful, their heads lowered a little menacingly, pale horns curving upwards.

Further away, a broader expanse of water blends invisibly into the horizon where a solitary lighthouse is picked out against the sky, matched further to the right by the silhouette of an ancient church tower crowned by battlements that were added as a protection against pirates some seven hundred years ago.

Close to the church stand painted gypsy caravans. Later, when the sun sinks, there will be the sound of flamenco guitars, with rhythmic clapping of hands and the swirl of jet-black hair and brilliant-coloured skirts around a camp-fire.

Scattered nearby are white reed-thatched houses, hunched low against the wind and with a cross raised above the roof. They are survivors of those lovingly drawn by Van Gogh and built for the cowboys who ride those white horses in the marshes and tend the black bulls.

A solitary horse grazing in a nearby field is quite unconcerned by the presence of two companions perched on its back; they are a pair of cattle egrets performing the useful service of removing ticks and horse-flies.

As evening settles in, the colours of the marshes deepen and the veil of heat hanging over the great lagoon lifts. Suddenly it is no longer an empty expanse of water: its vast spread is alive with scarlet flamingos, several thousand of them dotted across the shallows, their long necks lowered, curved beaks scooping beneath the surface for seafood. They are the true royalty of the Camargue.

In short, this broad triangle of the Rhône delta provides some of the richest breeding-grounds for wildlife in the entire western world. At the same time this mysterious patchwork of lagoon, marsh, scrub, salt-pans and rice-fields has also been another kind of breeding-ground: it has been the focus and inspiration for a wealth of legends and stories. It is a mythical landscape, and a romantic landscape. It has been seen as a Garden of Eden before the Fall, the idyllic survivor of a pre-industrial age where man and nature co-exist in harmony. It has been the nostalgic symbol of a free Provence before France annexed the region and crushed its culture. Two crusades were launched from here. Medieval monks came in search of the purity of the wilderness and built monasteries in the inhospitable marshes. Artists and writers have been drawn to the area to be touched by its magic and mystery. Gypsies from all over Europe gather every year to celebrate the festival of their patron saint, the black Sara. And it is the setting for one of the most poetic of Christian legends, that of the Three Marys who drifted here by open boat from the Holy Land following the Crucifixion, and whose arrival is celebrated annually in a procession in which their effigies are carried back into the sea from where they came.

I have a number of debts to acknowledge. Firstly to my wife, Anne Kelleher, the best of "in house" editors, who also accompanied me on exploratory treks across the baked Camargue salt-marshes, following the prints of horses' hooves and stooping to retrieve scarlet flamingos' feathers, which now adorn our mantelpiece. Then, to a long-time resident of the Camargue, Catherine Aldington, whom I first me in Provence many decades ago in our salad days, and who gave me invaluable introductions to local experts as well as keeping me up to date with local politics, local events and local gossip. To another old friend, the poet and novelist Jacques Temple, native of Montpellier, who loves this region and was among the first people to share it with me. To Alison Duncan, of the Ligue pour la Protection des Oiseaux, who kindly gave me an introduction to the Tour du Valat biological station. To my publisher at Signal Books, James Ferguson, who enjoys the Camargue as much as I do, and who urged me to write this book. Finally, I could never have undertaken such a task without the resources of that wonderful institution, the London Library, of which my late father gave me life membership as a twenty-first birthday present all those decades ago. So, to him I owe a very special posthumous debt of gratitude for one of the most rewarding gifts any writer could hope to receive.

London and Provence, 2008

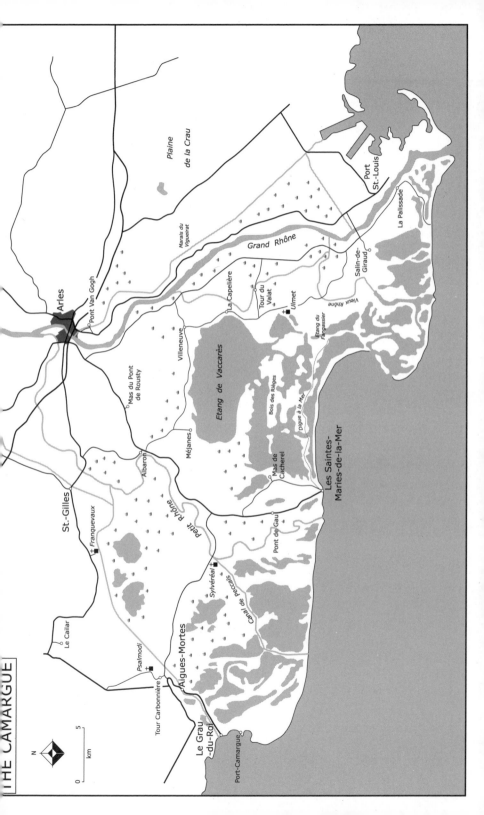

THE CAMARGUE

N

0   5
km

St.-Gilles

Le Cailar

Franquevaux

Psalmodi

Tour Carbonnière

Aigues-Mortes

Le Grau
-du-Roi

Port-Camargue

Sylvéréal

Canal de Peccaïs

Albaron

Petit Rhône

Méjanes

Pont de Gau

Mas de
Cacherel

Etang de Vaccarès

Bois des Rièges

Digue à la Mer

Les Saintes-
Maries-de-la-Mer

Villeneuve

Mas du Pont
de Rousty

La Capelière

Tour du
Valat

Ulmet

Etang du
Fangassier

Vieux Rhône

Salin-de-
Giraud

Grand Rhône

Marais du
Vigueirat

Pont Van Gogh

Arles

Plaine
de la Crau

Port
St.-Louis

La Palissade

Chapter One

THE RIVER

The story of the Camargue begins with the river.

Five hundred miles from its exit into the Mediterranean the Rhône is born as a mountain stream gushing from a glacier in the Swiss Alps at an altitude of well over six thousand feet. The stream travels along an Alpine valley north-west until it joins forces with lesser tributaries to create one of the largest freshwater lakes in Europe, Lake Geneva. Forty-five miles further to the west the river re-emerges at the far end of the lake, bisecting the city of Geneva before heading south-west into France. Leaving the mountains it is then joined at Lyon by the Saône, after which the Rhône flows directly south past Orange and Avignon until it approaches the former Roman city of Arles. Here it splits into two at a village appropriately named Fourques ("fork"). From this point, at the apex of a broad triangle, the entire area becomes a river delta, with the principal channel, the Grand Rhône, flowing south-east to enter the Mediterranean beyond Port St.-Louis, and the Petit Rhône describing a more leisurely journey south-west to enter the sea a little to the west of the coastal town of Les Saintes-Maries-de-la-Mer.

I

This triangular delta lying between the twin arms of the River Rhône, some three hundred square miles of it, is the Camargue—traditionally known as the "island", or *isclo* in the Provençal language (as it is wholly surrounded by water). In fact, the area broadly referred to as the Camargue is a good deal larger than this, the reason being that the two present branches of the river date back no further than the fifteenth century. Before that date, and for many thousands of years previously, the Rhône changed it various courses frequently, carving fresh channels through the sheer force of floodwater and covering a far wider area than it does now, many of these former branches surviving today as a network of canals and narrow waterways.

Accordingly the region we generally think of as the Camargue extends at least as far as Aigues-Mortes to the west and well beyond the Grand Rhône to the east, a total of roughly five hundred square miles. Contained within the *départements* of Bouches-du- Rhône, Gard and to a lesser extent Hérault, it is Western Europe's most extensive river delta. In all, it is an exceedingly large wilderness.

What the entire area has in common is its geological make-up. Two natural forces have created the Camargue: the river and the sea. Over many millennia the constantly-changing branches of the Rhône built up deposits of silt on the river-bed as they reached the Mediterranean, until eventually those deposits rose high enough to push the sea further and further back, so creating new tracts of land which in time became fertile where they were irrigated by rain and river-water, or else they remained salt-marsh with scattered islands where the sea continued to infiltrate.

This broadly speaking is the geological shape of the Camargue which we recognize today: a division between a fertile region in the northern part of the delta, and lagoons and salt-marsh predominating closer to the sea. Yet this geographical pattern is the product of many millennia of constant change, which became more or less stabilized only as recently as a century-and-a-half ago.

When this marshy wilderness was first inhabited by human beings is far from certain. Early in the First Millennium BC the first people to settle along the European coastline of the western Mediterranean—from Italy in the east as far as Spain in the west—are known to us as the Ligurians, a loose term masking the fact that we know practically nothing about them except that they seem to have lived in isolated pockets and acquired a reputation (probably unjustified) for being pirates. The Ligurians apparently subsisted chiefly by hunting and fishing, and given the quantity of wildfowl frequenting the Camargue wetlands today it is reasonable to assume that they took good advantage of so much food for free. Whether they actually lived in the delta itself rather than in the hinterland seems less likely. Since much of the region was an unhealthy and uninviting swamp they may well have preferred to establish their villages on firmer ground inland, making hunting forays into the swamplands in search of duck, game and fish.

Gradually the picture becomes a good deal clearer. We know that during the seventh century BC successive waves of settlers arrived from Greece, principally from Greek territories in Asia Minor from where they had been evicted by Persian invaders. These were not by and large farmers but sea people, many of them enterprising merchants who proceeded to set up trading stations along the coast, the principal one being named Massalia (which later became Marseille). Another trading post which the Greeks established was on a rocky outcrop at the northern tip of the Rhône delta overlooking the marshes, a settlement they called Theline (soon to become Arelate, and subsequently Arles). There were certainly other Greek settlements within the delta itself, including one on the site of what is now the Camargue "capital", Les Saintes-Maries-de-la-Mer, though the sole evidence of such a settlement consists of fragments of Greek pottery vessels which have been dredged up from the nearby lagoons. Not for the last time the fickle geography of the Camargue has proved adept at destroying its history.

Then came the Romans—and with them one of the first of many legends to have attached themselves to the Camargue. In the year 126 BC Rome received an urgent appeal by the local Ligurians for military support against marauding Celtic tribes from north of the Alps. The appeal was answered, and the Celts were duly routed by Roman military prowess. As was their wont the Romans took advantage of their victory and military presence by establishing a permanent settlement in the region, Aquae Sextiae, which ultimately became Aix-en-Provence. Two decades later an even more threatening Celtic invasion was quashed largely through the ingenuity of a Roman general by the name of Caius Marius. His success lay in having constructed a canal from the sea across the Camargue which was deep and broad enough to transport troops and military equipment inland. As a result the legend of Caius Marius as the local saviour was born, Marius becoming a popular boys' name in Provence, as it still is more than two thousand years later. It has even been claimed that the word Camargue is derived from the name of the great Roman general: *Caii Marii ager*, meaning "the field of Caius Marius". There are, however, more convincing candidates for the origin of the name, among them a Roman country gentleman called Aulus Annius Camars who owned a large estate called "L'Insula Camarica" and who is reputed to have been the first man to herd the celebrated Camargue white horses for use in the games held in the Roman arenas. A marble fragment with an inscription in his honour is displayed in the Museum of the Camargue (about which more later in this chapter).

Stepping from legend back into history, in the year 46 BC the Romans established a colony in the former Greek settlement of Arelate, at the northern tip of the Rhône delta. Three years later the fortunes of the place, and of the Camargue as a whole, took a dramatic turn when Julius Caesar's army defeated that of his rival in the Roman civil war, Pompey the Great. The crucial issue was that Arelate, by now a prosperous and largely independent community, had taken Caesar's side in the conflict, supplying ships and military help, whereas the great port of Massalia had supported Pompey. Thereafter Massalia was humbled into second-class status, stripped of its wealth and possessions, while privileges were poured on to Arelate by the grateful Caesar. He ordered twenty warships to be built there, and settled six thousand veterans of the 6th Roman Legion in the area. Arelate became "Little Rome in Gaul", at the very heart of Caesar's new province—his *Provincia*: hence the title "Provence". And so Arles/Arelate continued to flourish. The awesome Roman monuments which still dominate the centre of the modern city date from the decades following Julius Caesar's munificent acts of patronage: principally the amphitheatre, which was used for religious ceremonies and for bloody gladiatorial contests, and was the largest outside Italy, capable of holding 25,000 spectators; and the nearby semicircular theatre, built under Augustus Caesar and designed for dramatic performances, which could comfortably seat an audience of 10,000.

In short, within the space of less than a century Arles/Arelate had become expansive, powerful and wealthy.

It is intriguing to speculate on the effect this explosion of affluence may have had on the Camargue itself, which after all lay on the new city's very doorstep. Firm evidence is in short supply, but significant nonetheless. For instance, Julius Caesar's reward to Arles of the commission to build twenty warships would have meant a demand for large quantities of the appropriate hard-wood, notably oak, which would not have been easily available in the inland regions immediately to the north of the city, mostly given over to scrubby areas of pine and other softwood. So where did Arles get its oak from? It has been suggested (with more confidence than information) that the rich alluvial soil deposited in the Rhône delta over such an enormous span of time had resulted in the establishment of dense forests of wood of a kind that would have been ideally suited for ship-building, and that as a result whole areas of the Camargue were now deforested for this purpose.

This can be little more than surmise—and yet surmise which rests on intriguing circumstantial evidence. The freshwater regions of the Camargue today still possess areas of dense woodlands made up of a variety of trees that include several species of oak, which makes it highly likely that before intensive cultivation large parts of the delta may well have been much more thickly forested than they are now. We also know that those six thousand veteran legionnaires whom Caesar settled in the region were awarded plots of land, and that in a relatively short space of time the Camargue was being described by Caesar in his *Commentaries* as being the granary of the Roman armies in Gaul. It seems a reasonable supposition that those legionnaires cleared forests to supply wood for Caesar's warships, and that they also became successful farmers, reaping the benefits of soil regularly irrigated by the Rhône in precisely the way the Nile annually irrigated the land of Egypt. And just as Egypt became the granary of Rome, so the Camargue became the granary of the Roman *Provincia*.

Clearly these new farmers of the Camargue prospered mightily. It is known that, being good Romans, they were responsible for constructing the first roads across the drier parts of the Camargue, and that they also built themselves spacious villas on higher ground (a relative term when applied to the Rhône delta, meaning any land a few feet or so above marsh level). Sadly, in such a geologically unstable territory none of their villas has survived, not even the customary foundations and sophisticated drainage and heating systems we have come to expect from Roman sites: only coins and fragments of pottery. In the city of Arles the Musée de l'Arles Antique presents an overall picture of Roman life in the *Provincia* at this time—under the imperial gaze of a colossal statue of Augustus Caesar—but is short on specific records of contemporary rural life in the delta itself.

However, deep in the Camargue there survives an eloquent testimony to the Roman dedication to farming. Midway between the two arms of the Rhône, and eight miles to the south-west of Arles, is the Mas du Pont de Rousty, standing amid open fields and reed-lined dykes reminiscent of the English fen-country. *Mas* is the Provençal word for a farmhouse or a cluster of farm buildings, and the Mas du Pont de Rousty is a handsome example of the kind of farm that is traditional to the Camargue, consisting of a group of long low buildings arranged round a central space, all turning their backs on the north wind that regularly scythes through the delta at all seasons, known—with little affection—as the mistral.

Close to the *mas* lies a stretched-out farm-building which since 1979 has been converted into the Musée de la Camargue (Museum of the Camargue). Originally it was the farm's sheepfold, its sheer length an indication of the size of the flocks that were once housed in it, though only during winter. For the summer months the sheep of the Camargue were (and still are) driven to mountain pastures by shepherds to the accompaniment of sheep-bells and the patter of many thousands of delicate feet on village cobblestones in the stillness of the night—a traditional journey known as the transhumance. No one who has witnessed this extraordinary nocturnal passage of animals through the hill-villages of the Cévennes is unlikely ever to forget it.

But down in the Museum of the Camargue, along with displays demonstrating various aspects of rural life—agriculture, stock rearing, hunting, fishing, domestic day-to-day business—is the mutilated stone statue of a god which tells an important story about rural life here in Roman times. Had the statue been complete its identity would have been startlingly evident from even the furthest part of the building, because the god in question was none other than Priapus whose most notable attribute was a sexual organ of heroic proportions. Whether or not his missing member is now a cherished collector's item somewhere, or is locked away in the vaults of a *musée lapidaire*, the presence of the god here in the Camargue, where the statue was found, is deeply significant. In rural areas Priapus was worshipped not as a symbol of male boastfulness but as a god of fertility as it applied to an agricultural community; he was a guardian of the forests, rivers and fields. He was the deity of farmers, his mighty presence offering assurance to them that the Camargue would continue to be, as Julius Caesar had claimed, the granary of Roman Gaul.

The centuries following the collapse of the Roman Empire in the fifth century were Dark Ages in the Rhône delta just as they were elsewhere in Europe. Over a period of four hundred years the former Roman city of Arles suffered at least ten major sieges—from Visigoths, Franks, Ostrogoths, and latterly from wave upon wave of Saracen marauders sweeping up from North Africa and the recently-conquered regions of the Spanish peninsula. The Camargue seems to have become more or less uninhabited. These were centuries of decay. The comfortable villas built by those Roman legionnaires who had become successful farmers were now deserted, gradually crumbling away or becoming engulfed by the ever-shifting channels of the Rhône. Those branches of the river which once transported corn and military supplies for the Roman armies now became convenient arteries for conveying pirates inland to Arles and other low-lying towns and settlements on the northern fringes of the delta. The Camargue in the Dark Ages was no place to farm or hunt, least of all to build a house to live in.

Besides the Rhône there was a second river which played its part in creating this bleak wilderness. Beyond what is now the Grand Rhône lies the most easterly stretch of marshland and lagoons known as the Grand Plan du Bourg, which is geologically part of the Camargue without officially being so. Immediately beyond this area lies one of the most desolate and uninviting regions in Western Europe. This is the plain of the Crau, much of which is little more than a landscape of stones, inhabited by the occasional flock of sheep and hopeful ornithologist seeking some of the rare birds who inhabit the place. It could hardly be more different from the Camargue which adjoins it. But, like the Camargue, it has attracted it legends, and the most striking of these offers a colourful mythological explanation for the Crau's arid appearance. It concerns the Greek hero Hercules. Having completed the tenth of his twelve labours—the theft of the cattle of Geryon—Hercules was passing this way driving his loot peacefully back towards Greece when he was set upon by an armed force of Ligurians who attempted to steal the hero's cattle. His response, armed with only a club, was to take on the mob single-handed, offering as he did so a prayer to his father (a useful parent to have in such circumstances, being Zeus). As a result the king of the gods sent down a vast storm of stones, which had the effect of putting the surprised Ligurians to flight.

The true explanation for the barren stoniness of the Crau is more prosaic. The area is actually the dried river-bed of the Durance, a river which rises in the southern Alps and nowadays flows westwards across Provence to join the Rhône a little south of Avignon. But for most of its existence the Durance flowed directly into the Mediterranean more or less in parallel to the Rhône and a little to the east. It is a puzzling trick of geology that two sister rivers, both rising in the Alps and both heading in the same direction southwards, should end their journeys quite so differently, one as a marsh, the other as a desert.

The Durance altered its course only once—dramatically—whereas the various veins of the Rhône remained erratic for most of its existence right up until the late Middle Ages. By this time the landscape of the Camargue was undergoing further changes. Measures were being taken, somewhat belatedly, to protect Arles and other townships in the region from pirate attacks which had been going on for almost a thousand years, ever since the collapse of Roman authority. Towers began to be raised on the river-banks along the different branches of the Rhône, and these in turn encouraged and protected small agricultural settlements. One of the earliest of these settlements was at Albaron, today an unremarkable cluster of more recent buildings overlooking a sharp bend in the Petit Rhône halfway between Arles and the sea, but none the less retaining its fortified tower begun as early as the thirteenth century. Other medieval towers still punctuate the landscape of the Camargue here and there, the best-preserved being the fourteenth-century Tour Carbonnière, which straddles a minor road (the D46) running north a short distance from the fortress-town of Aigues-Mortes (about which more in Chapters 5 and 6).

So, as the geography of the delta eventually stabilized, and the threats of piracy and invasion at last receded, human life started to return to the marshlands. One crucial step towards that end took place during the early decades of the eighteenth century: the hugely ambitious task of attempting to seal the twin branches of the Rhône. This led ultimately to the construction of substantial river-banks along both sides of the Grand and Petit Rhône, a task finally completed only after the building of the sea-dyke in the mid-nineteenth century. But once constructed, these embankments not only put an end to the unpredictable flooding by the swollen river which had been a regular occurrence in the delta; they also made it possible to keep the sea out of the more inland stretches of salt-marsh, and hence to enable a system of controlled irrigation of these areas to be set up with fresh river-water drawn from directly the Rhône. As a result, broad areas of the Camargue began to become rich fertile land once more, just as they had been when the Romans employed their own remarkable engineering skills to control the fickle waters of the delta and make the Camargue the granary of Gaul.

The eighteenth- and nineteenth-century feat of controlling the temper of the Rhône meant that the wilderness years were finally over, and from this point onwards agriculture and stock-breeding began to transform much of the landscape of the Camargue into something approaching what it is today. Farming flourished once again, and so did the farmers. Before long substantial farmhouses with their adjoining barns and other outbuildings started to appear right across the newly-irrigated lands of the delta. It is estimated that at least two hundred such *mas* were built in the Camargue from the time when the twin branches of the Rhône began to be embanked during the eighteenth century. Most of these farms still exist; a close inspection of any detailed map of the Rhône delta reveals the word *mas* scattered everywhere you look across the open spaces, even though on the ground they are often invisible, hidden within thickets of dense woodland planted chiefly as a barrier against the mistral, which scours the Provençal landscape unpredictably, sometimes for weeks on end.

There are no more than fragmentary records of the Camargue during this long period; merely legal documents relating to land ownership with the odd personal observation thrown in, often of a derogatory nature relating to the mosquitoes or the general unhealthiness of the climate. Then in the following century, the nineteenth, we begin to receive eye-witness accounts of the Camargue from visiting writers.

The Digue à la Mer, "like a walk along the rim of the world."

Poets and novelists of the Romantic era became eager to answer the call of the wild. Like the Alps, here was an area which could offer artists the thrill of the sublime. Among the earliest writers to head south for the delta was Alexandre Dumas (*père*). The celebrated author of *The Three Musketeers* and *The Count of Monte Cristo* duly set out to exploit this new vogue for "nature" by keeping a travel journal, which in 1851 he published as *Pictures of Travel in the South of France* (see Chapter 6). As it transpired, the financial rewards of the enterprise failed to match Dumas' expectations, and any thrill of the sublime he may have experienced proved no compensation for the discomforts he was compelled to endure. One of these was the mistral, which he found a particular horror: "instead of penetrating the body through the skin, it seizes on the marrow of the bones, and paralyses one." As for the landscape generally, "the country may be considered as somewhat peculiar", he noted stuffily. But he then got into his stride. The Camargue was, he explained to his Parisian readers, "an immense swamp over which the sea rolled some two thousand years ago, but from which it appears to have receded"—though he hardly sounded convinced. In short he pronounced the whole area to be "uninhabited and uninhabitable".

It was by now, of course, neither of these things. The farming communities were already well established, as were the small townships of Les Saintes-Maries-de-la-Mer and Aigues-Mortes.

Five years after Dumas published his disgruntled journal a natural disaster struck the delta. Exceptionally heavy storms caused the banks of the Rhône near the coast to be breached, so letting in massive quantities of both river- and sea-water which flooded the entire area as far inland as twelve miles, drowning numerous herds of bulls and white horses in the process. But now there was help. The Camargue was by this time "on the map" in Paris. Enough celebrities had visited the region to make politicians conscious of its uniqueness and its special appeal; in consequence the sheer scale of this new catastrophe had the effect of stirring the French state into action. And in the following year, 1857, the authorities undertook to finance the building of a sea-wall 28 miles in length and more than six feet high. This was the Digue à la Mer, and it ran—as it still does—eastwards from close to Les Saintes-Maries-de-la-Mer between the sand-dunes on one side and dozens of small lagoons, reed-beds and wooded islands on the other. Today the *digue* provides a lonely and spectacularly beautiful walk for the intrepid traveller through some of the most remote stretches of the Camargue. Here, under enormous skies and with a horizon speckled with scarlet flamingos and white egrets, it can feel like a walk along the rim of the world.

The twentieth century contributed its share of alarms and threats to the geography of the delta. The largest of the lagoons in the Camargue is the Etang de Vaccarès, now the centre of the Réserve Nationale de Camargue, which covers 32,000 acres and is one of the best-protected areas for wildlife in all of France. Yet over a period of several years between the two world wars the water level in the Vaccarès dropped steadily, until by the late-1920s it had become so low that covetous eyes began to peer at such a vast area going to waste, and serious plans were drawn up over glasses of *pastis* and much Gauloise smoke to drain it for the purposes of agriculture.

This was a touch-and-go period for the Camargue, and had these venal plans been put into practice the Rhône delta would today be just another low-lying area of farmland over which the occasional heron lazily flaps. In the end the crisis was averted not by any public-spirited vision of a wildlife paradise but by hard-nosed commercial rivalry. The consortium of companies producing sea-salt in the nearby area between the Vaccarès and the Mediterranean—at that time the largest such operation in Europe—were becoming alarmed by the prospect of extensive new areas of agricultural land irrigated by river-water encroaching on territories covered by sea-water and given over to the production of sea salt. With the threat of financial pain hanging over them they succeeded in purchasing the Vaccarès lagoon along with much of the surrounding marshland simply in order to protect their own commercial interests. They then had the wit to offer the management (though not the ownership) of the entire area to a body of well-meaning naturalists in Paris who called themselves the Société Nationale d'Acclimatisation de France. The naturalists seem to have been more than a little surprised to find such bounty falling suddenly into their laps, and it took some time for a body of Parisian academics and philanthropists to produce a workable response. None the less a sense of purpose and a need for urgent action prevailed, and in 1929 the Camargue nature reserve became a reality, owing its existence to nothing more noble than its provision of a convenient barrier between the commercial interests of salt to the south of it and farming to the north.

It was at this stage that the geography of the Rhône came into its own. The water level of the Vaccarès had fallen drastically during the 1920s: hence so much talk of draining it for the purposes of agriculture. Now, in its proposed transformation into a nature reserve a system of fresh-water irrigation was essential if the great lagoon was not to become a mere mud-bath. In answer to this challenge the management of the new reserve set about installing pumping stations to draw water from the Grand Rhône, which ran only a short distance to the east of the Vaccarès. They were also able for irrigation purposes to make use of one of the former courses of the river which had been isolated ever since the embanking of the Rhône more than two centuries earlier. This ran even closer to the lagoon, and is still recorded on modern maps under the name Vieux Rhône.

With new pumping stations, and the consequent ability to control the level of water, as well as a balance between salt and fresh water, the new Vaccarès came into being. And with its incorporation into a new nature reserve, the Camargue began to appear more or less the region we recognize today, casting a blind eye at the lava-flow of the modern tourist industry. Even so, nature still has a way of dramatically reasserting itself. In December 2003 the level of the Rhône rose to a record level after torrential rains and the river burst its banks in several places. Worst-hit was the town of St.-Gilles, on the edge of the Camargue, where flood-waters engulfed a huge area of land, claiming several lives.

Such occasional disasters notwithstanding, after so many centuries and millennia of constant disturbance and change, the great delta finally settled down into—roughly speaking—three distinct regions. Along the sea-shore runs a long range of sand-dunes keeping out the ocean, constantly changing though it is with the assault of the mistral from the north and storms boiling up from the Mediterranean southwards. Protected by these undulating hills of sand, and by the long sea dyke, lies a surreal landscape of salt-pans carefully irrigated by the sea, all set out in a precise grid pattern with slender tracks running between them like strips of lead in a stained-glass window.

Furthest from this sea area, the more northerly region of the Camargue is given over to woodland, pasture and cultivation. Here is where the celebrated Camargue black bulls graze in the fields and raise their heads imperiously as you pass, and where the low-lying farms (the *mas*) hide out of sight within dense clusters of trees, their windows south-facing, their north-facing walls often windowless against the wind. This is the region the Romans once made the granary of Gaul. Now, since the Second World War, the principal crop is rice, including the distinctive Camargue red rice, its colour being that of the outer layer of the unpolished grain. The irrigated paddy-fields make the area effectively an extension of the nature reserve, with herons and white egrets stalking for grubs among the rows of young rice plants, while in adjoining meadows a recent arrival, the yellow-plumed cattle egret, chooses a drier meal in the shape of ticks systematically plucked from the backs of white horses grazing there quite unconcerned.

Then, between these two contrasting regions lies the central area of the delta, 16,000 acres of it, which in most people's eyes is the most recognizable face of the Camargue, though it is actually more diverse in character than the other two regions, as well as varying greatly season by season. This is the moody and romantic landscape that visitors cherish. There are miles of salt-marsh, much of which dries out in the summer months, leaving expanses of mud cracked by the heat and bearing the imprint of horses' hooves and a scattering of scarlet flamingo feathers. Here and there the marsh is crisscrossed with raised dykes used as footpaths and horse trails; and between them are thickets of dense reed-bed raucous with nesting marsh-birds, and countless half-hidden lagoons where herons and other wading birds stalk for food and white horses break cover to head for the next small island.

Beyond this mosaic of mud and water spreads the Vaccarès itself, the heart of the Réserve Nationale de Camargue. Here is a lagoon vast enough to make the far shore invisible except for a distant lighthouse and a line of inaccessible islands, called the Bois des Rièges, which are home to wild boar as well as to some of Europe's rarest trees. Rarer still in the Bois des Rièges is the ghostly presence of one of the Camargue's many colourful legends, a half-human creature first seen (and indeed last seen) back in the fifteenth century. This is the celebrated Beast of the Vaccarès, about which there will be more to say in a later chapter.

The Camargue is a landscape which breeds legends of all kinds, and one of the most potent and moving of these came into being only a few miles from the Vaccarès along the coast to the west, at a place which bears the name of that legend, Les Saintes-Maries-de-la-Mer.

Chapter Two

THE SAINTS FROM THE SEA

Gaze across the broad lagoons of the Camargue towards the sea and a hulk of a building breaks the skyline. It is jagged with battlements, though it is not a fortress but a medieval church—with protective armour added—and it rises massively above the rooftops of the small coastal town of Les Saintes-Maries-de-la-Mer, unofficial capital of the Camargue, of which this fearsome chunk of masonry is the parish church.

Approaching closer, the building begins to look less like a fortress than an ungainly ship which has somehow got beached here and left high and dry. And as it happens, the image of a ship could hardly be more appropriate. This is a town which owes its fame and prosperity to a Provençal legend relating to figures close to Jesus Christ who miraculously arrived here from the sea. And the church of Les Saintes-Maries is its shrine.

The principal source of the legend is a highly imaginative account of the lives of the saints (nearly two hundred of them all told) called *La*

Légende Dorée (*The Golden Legend*), which was compiled by an eminent Dominican cleric and chronicler by the name of Jacques de Voragine in the thirteenth century. The story, as best it can be pieced together, is this. After the Crucifixion the detractors of Christ are said to have continued their vendetta by placing members of His family and followers in an open boat without sails or oars, and setting it adrift from the coast of Palestine. They consisted of Mary Salome, who was the mother of the apostles James and John, Mary Jacob, the sister of the Virgin Mary, and Mary Magdalene. Also with them were the Magdalene's own sister Martha and her brother Lazarus, Christ's close friend whom He had brought back from the dead. In addition, the hapless crew included the more shadowy figures of Saints Maximin and Sidonius, as they later became known, along with the even more shadowy figure of Sara, who is said to have been the Egyptian servant of Mary Salome and Mary Jacob. In all there was a complement of eight.

The Boat of Bethany, as it became known (named after Lazarus' birthplace near Jerusalem and where Jesus had often stayed), drifted westwards from Palestine until the winds and currents—and doubtless the hand of God—guided the vessel to a desolate stretch of shore in what is now the Camargue. The only sign of human habitation was a Greek fortress, and here Mary Salome and Mary Jacob, together with their servant Sara, took refuge and built a small oratory, so establishing the first Christian community in the western Mediterranean. Meanwhile the younger, more vigorous members of the party set out to spread the gospel among the unsuspecting Ligurians, the native inhabitants of the region. Lazarus headed eastwards for the Greek port of Massalia (where he became its first bishop). Maximin and Sidonius journeyed inland to what is now Aix-en-Provence, while Martha travelled northwards to Tarascon where she successfully tamed a predatory dragon living in the Rhône, leading the meek creature through the streets of the town where the inhabitants proceeded to stone it to death. As for Mary Magdalene, she was guided by an angel to a grotto where she apparently remained in a state of continual prayer until her death thirty-five years later.

This in outline is the story as it has come down to us. Setting aside its multiple absurdities, what is intriguing is trying to trace how such a legend came into being, where it may have come from, and why it should be focused on the Camargue rather than anywhere else. There are a few guidelines in such a search, and with the aid of some semantic archaeology a pattern begins to emerge.

The Golden Legend, written in Italy, was one of the most popular religious works of the Middle Ages, much copied and much translated from the original Latin. It was compiled during the high noon of medieval Christianity and church-building—the era of Gothic cathedrals and soaring hopes for a better world and an even better heaven. A resurgent Christianity was reaching out to embrace whatever could be found to fill those long dark centuries between the time of Christ and the present age. It was an embrace that added colour, authenticity and historical credentials to the Christian story. *The Golden Legend* fulfilled all these requirements; it supplied in a single work an all-embracing family history for the Christian world. In the cause of proselytizing it was the perfect tool.

It is in the nature of legends to grow and adapt themselves, chameleon-like, according to need, and the legend of the Three Marys is no exception. So, when and how did it first appear, and how did it subsequently evolve?

We know that a Roman writer in the fourth century describes a settlement in what is now the Camargue by the name of *Oppidium Priscum Ra*, and that an early Christian church was established here at about the same time. This is not hard to believe since nearby Arelate (later Arles) was at this time the favourite city of the first Christian Roman emperor, Constantine 1, and that the city effectively governed the entire western part of the Roman Empire, including Spain, Gaul and even as far north as Brittany. Three centuries had already passed since Julius Caesar described the Camargue as the granary of Roman Gaul. And since *priscus* means "ancient" or "first", it seems clear that Oppidum Priscum Ra had been a settlement for some considerable period of time, and that being on the sea it must have been a port of some description, no doubt servicing the prosperous and important city of Arelate, with the Rhône as its chief means of communication.

So far, so good, but why *Ra*? It is not a Latin word. So where might it come from? It may seem a red herring to mention it, but *Râ* is actually the name of the supreme deity of ancient Egypt, the sun-god. And since Egypt formed part of the Roman Empire at this time, and the Romans were in the habit of borrowing their gods from the territories they conquered, it is not improbable that Râ became the adopted deity watching over the affairs of this small maritime settlement in the Mediterranean sun: none of which, admittedly, casts even the dimmest light on the legend of the Three Marys.

What does, however, cast light on that legend is the fact that the first Christian church to be erected here is known to have been built on the site of a Roman temple dedicated to three sea-goddesses. The temple was erected over a spring of fresh water (which still exists beneath the present church in Les Saintes-Maries). By the sixth century, according to the then Bishop of Arles, this same church had acquired a dedication to "Sainte-Marie-de-Ratis". Suddenly two entirely new factors have entered the equation. The word *Ratis* was a Provençal mistranslation of *Ra*, taken now to mean "raft", or "boat". The Egyptian sun-god has becomes a vessel. And we have Mary as well. It is far from clear which Mary the dedication referred to, or how she became attached to the place. None the less what does become evident is that the framework of the legend which seven centuries later came to be expanded in *The Golden Legend* was already present. In other words, a Roman cult involving the worship of three sea-goddesses has become Christianized into the story of three followers of Jesus arriving by sea, while a far earlier cult revolving around the Egyptian sun-god led to the god's name, Ra, becoming misinterpreted to mean the raft or boat on which the Three Marys drifted here from the Holy Land.

So, from a hotchpotch of pagan myths one of the most endearing and enduring of Christian legends was born—one which gave this small coastal town in the Camargue its name, and helped make it celebrated throughout the Christian world. Such is the alchemy of myth-making.

Yet the legend does not rest there. The medieval church soon discovered ways in which elements of the story of the Three Marys could be expanded to its own considerable advantage. How it did so was by exploiting the universal popular belief in the spiritual power of holy relics, and of course taking advantage of the credulity of those who flocked in their thousands to venerate those relics on display in churches. The two figures in the story of the Marys who came to serve the interests of the church most fruitfully were Mary Magdalene and her brother Lazarus. In short, as though by divine guidance, more than a thousand years after the supposed arrival of the Boat of Bethany on the remote shores of the Camargue, the bones of both Lazarus and Mary Magdalene were found—or so it was claimed.

This "discovery" needs to be put in the context of the times. In the early Middle Ages the founding and financing of abbeys and other church establishments depended to a very large extent on the donations of visiting pilgrims, rich and poor. The size of these contributions tended to be in proportion to the status of the relics owned by the institutions concerned. Putting it in modern investment terms, a preserved fragment of the Holy Cross would be worth millions in terms of annual income to a monastery, whereas the fingernail of a minor saint might only be worth a few thousand. The possession of important relics was like having the ear of God; pilgrims would journey far and pay handsomely for the opportunity to have their prayers listened to. Not surprisingly there was a brisk trade in acquiring such relics, as well as a great deal of skullduggery in the process. The former abbey of Conques, on the southern edge of the central *massif* of France, grew rich and powerful on the strength of possessing some of the most revered relics in Christendom (the *Trésor de Ste.-Foi*, as it is known today). Yet Conques had no historical right to them whatever: the abbey only managed to acquire them by planting one of its monks in the nearby monastery of Agen, and who after ten years of waiting for an opportunity finally made off with the holy loot one evening while the community was in the rectory at dinner. Then there is the story of a pious traveller who was visiting shrines in France being shown the skull of John the Baptist on two successive days, the custodian of the second monastery offering by way of an explanation that the relic which the visitor had seen the previous day must have been the skull of the saint as a young man.

The embroidering of the stories of Mary Magdalene and Lazarus lacks any such bare-faced cynicism: none the less it has its roots in a similar naïveté on the part of the citizenry as a whole which allowed medieval church leaders to encourage people to believe more or less what it suited them to believe. Credulity was everything, for abbey and pilgrim alike. Mary Magdalene was long believed to have been buried close to her grotto in Provence. Even so, on the basis of no evidence of any value the monks of the Burgundian abbey of Vézelay then claimed that some bones which had come into their in possession were indeed those of the Magdalene. As a result, in the eleventh and twelfth centuries the abbey grew to become one of the most important centres of pilgrimage in the whole of France, and in consequence extremely rich.

As for Lazarus, his supposed remains underwent a similar journey to fame. After becoming the first bishop of Marseille Lazarus was martyred—his second death!—and there is no reliable account of where he is supposed to have been buried. But at much the same time as Mary Magdalene's remains miraculously reappeared in Vézelay another religious community in Burgundy, at Autun, claimed to have been presented with the remains of Lazarus, as a result of which a magnificent new cathedral was built, dedicated to the saint.

Disreputable or merely disingenuous? Beyond dispute is that without the opportunist fantasies of those churchmen two of the supreme masterpieces of church architecture and sculpture in medieval Europe would never have been created. Though several hundreds miles distant from the Camargue, the Basilica of St. Mary Magdalene at Vézelay and the Cathedral of St. Lazarus at Autun both owe their magnificent existence to the legend of the Three Marys.

And as such they stand as two golden footnotes to the story of the Camargue.

The fortified church at Les Saintes-Maries has been witness to a violent and bizarre history. The present church dates from the twelfth century, with its bristling battlements added two centuries later—for very good reason. But if ones eye can manage to blot out the battlements for a while, then the original church begins to look a great deal les ferocious. Its decorative band of blind arches running round the entire building is typical of the work of those itinerant Lombard stonemasons whose skills and sensibilities added elegant touches like these to so many Romanesque churches in central and southern France at this time. The fact that a Lombard workshop must have been based here in the un-inviting swamps while the church was being designed and built is itself an indication of the prestige which the legend of the Three Marys had already conferred on the place.

The original oratory built on this site by two of the three women is best regarded as wishful fiction unless one chooses to believe the story of the Boat of Bethany to be literally true. Even so, when the Roman armies arrived only a few decades after the magical boat the oratory would certainly have been replaced by the temple which we know they dedicated to three sea-goddesses. Then, after the Roman conversion to Christianity, this temple in turn would have made way for the first Christian church, probably during the fourth century at the time of Emperor Constantine, the first Christian Roman emperor, and it is this church which is likely to be the one described in the sixth century as being dedicated to St.-Mary-of-the-Raft (*Ratis*).

Three centuries later, this early church became the setting for an episode of macabre comedy—one that has doubtless been richly em-bellished in the telling over many centuries. However, this is the rich tale as it has come down to us. Following the Muslim conquest of most of Spain, Saracen raids throughout this entire southern region of France became repeated and deadly. Nowhere was safe. Arles itself was fre-quently sacked, and the original church at Les Saintes-Maries was destroyed, or at least partially so. Subsequently, during the course of re-construction, the church was formally visited by the Archbishop of Arles (by now no longer a mere bishopric). Unfortunately his tour of in-spection was abruptly terminated when a band of Saracens arrived on the scene and took him prisoner, demanding a substantial ransom to secure his release. This demand was agreed by the helpless Christian authorities. But in the meanwhile the unfortunate archbishop died, ap-parently of natural causes, or perhaps of shock. The resourceful Saracens, however, were not to be done out of their fat ransom. They honoured the agreement they had made with the Christians by hand-somely dressing up the defunct cleric and propping him beneath a canopy for all to see, with his eyes closed as though he were deep in holy thoughts. The ransom duly changed hands, and the raiders rapidly took their leave. They were already out of sight with their loot before the church representatives discovered that their revered archbishop was not lost in spiritual meditation after all.

A further two and a half centuries were to pass before work on the present church began, early in the twelfth century. Apart from the design and scale of the building another measure of the prestige by now enjoyed by Les Saintes-Maries as a pilgrimage centre is the fact that the new church, instead of being constructed of whatever local materials might be available, was built of sandstone quarried far inland and shipped down the Rhône from Arles at what must have been consider-able expense. The result is one of the masterpieces of Provençal Romanesque architecture, its militant appearance from the outside masking a darkly handsome interior with its elegant barrel-vaulted nave and finely-sculpted capitals surmounting the semi-circle of blind arches beyond the choir.

Several centuries later a single historic event was to elevate the fame and prestige of this new church to stratospheric heights. In 1448 Count René of Provence ("Good King René" as he is popularly la-belled, since he was also the titular king of Naples) ordered an excava-tion beneath the church in the area of the high altar. The purpose of the excavation was to put to the test the pious belief that here was where Mary Jacob and Mary Salome must have erected their original altar, and where it was also likely that that they themselves had been buried, along with their servant Sara. King René's convictions proved to be well-founded: bones were indeed found buried on either side of the present altar. Furthermore, they were said to have given off a sweet odour as they were unearthed, conclusive proof of their authenticity, so it was claimed.

No further evidence was required to convince René and all who were present at the scene of the excavation that here were undoubtedly the remains of Christ's family and followers. The relics were ceremonially washed in white wine before being sanctified by the Bishop of Marseille. "Good King René" himself ordered them to be placed in reliquaries in the upper chapel of the church. In addition a marble slab which had been discovered during the same excavation was deemed to be the very altar used by the first Christian community, having been placed there by the two Marys. These were awe-inspiring finds. And from these apocalyptic events were born the ceremonies and rituals which today characterize the life of Les Saintes-Maries-de-la-Mer, and have brought it fame.

René proceeded to award the town special tax exemptions and other privileges which he considered appropriate to so important a pilgrimage centre. Furthermore, dates were fixed for holding annual celebrations of the two saints whose remains supposedly now resided within the church: 24 May was declared to be the saint's day of Mary Jacob, while 22 October was the date given to the celebrations of Mary Salome.

Four and a half centuries later these are still the two dates when this small town by the sea goes wild. But before joining in these annual festivities it is important to introduce the most colourful figure to feature in the historic carnivals—one who so far has received only a passing mention in the story of the Camargue. None the less she is central to this story, and without her the Camargue would be a more sombre place. She is the servant who accompanied Mary Jacob and Mary Salome on the Boat of Bethany, and who remained with them after they landed here. She is the enigmatic Sara.

She is the reason why the roads leading to Les Saintes-Maries-de-la-Mer towards the end of May become choked with camper-vans, painted caravans and an eccentric assortment of battered jalopies bearing mainly Spanish or Eastern European number-plates, often with cooking-pots clanging from the rear doors, and sometimes a tethered goat trotting behind.

She is why the sizzling of roasting meat on open fires and the sound of flamenco guitars fill the hour of dusk across the fringes of the town on those evenings late in May.

She is why nobody walking the narrow streets of Les Saintes-Maries in the midday heat can avoid having the palm of one hand clutched firmly while beguiling assurances of fortune and romance are offered for the price of a few euros by a dusky figure clanging with beads and flashing a gold smile.

And—most of all—she is why Les Saintes-Maries-de-la-Mer has grown rich on the crowds who come to soak up the atmosphere of all this, and why the town itself sports a fashionable marina on the very spot where Van Gogh sat and sketched the painted fishing-boats drawn up along the shore.

Sara is the patron of gypsies. And each year, in May, thousands of her followers congregate here from all parts of Europe to venerate her and to join in the dramatic ceremony of the sea in which her effigy plays such an important part.

But who exactly was Sara?

In this land of myth and legend it should come as no surprise that there are several alternative accounts of her origin and identity from which you can take your pick. The version favoured by the church as well as by the tourist industry is the one consistent with the Boat of Bethany story, namely that Sara was the faithful servant of two of the Marys, and that she was apparently Egyptian, which accounts for her invariably being depicted as having a dark or dusky skin. A second version carries somewhat more plausibility, which is that Sara was herself a gypsy—very possibly a tribal chief—who lived in the area of the lower Rhône and gave protection to the Marys when they drifted ashore, remaining with them thereafter as a convert to Christianity.

A dramatic extension of this version of the story traces all gypsies back to a common homeland in India, describing Sara as Sara-la-Kali, the word *Kali* being of Sanskrit origin meaning "black", but also relating her to the Hindu goddess Kali, whose consort was the lord Siva. However, since the goddess Kali is described in one highly reputable encyclopedia as "a hideous, black-faced hag smeared with blood... naked except for her ornaments, consisting of a garland of skulls and a girdle of severed hands," it may be best to turn a blind eye to Sara's theoretical origins in Indian mythology, and to focus instead on the Sara we have here in the Camargue. Her effigy is mounted in the crypt of the church of Les Saintes-Maries-de-la-Mer, an impassive blue-robed figure awash with floral offerings and surrounded by a forest of candles. It is this effigy which is venerated by gypsies the world over as she awaits her annual ceremonial return to the sea.

Her special day is 24 May. The Catholic Church in its pragmatic wisdom decreed as recently as the 1930s that since gypsies were by and large devout Christians, and they also considerably outnumbered the pilgrims who come to venerate the relics of the Marys, then Sara should be permitted to share the great May festivities of the saints. Hence she is now welcomed in, and if she does not exactly steal the show the occasion would be a good deal plainer without her.

On this her special day, crowds have been building up in Les Saintes-Maries for the best part of a week, and by mid-morning the church is already crammed, as are the open spaces surrounding it. There is a buzz about the place, an air of expectation and of fiesta—music on every street-corner, singing and laughter, cafés bursting at the seams, colourful gypsy dresses dotted among the crowds, tourist cameras held high on periscopes, fortune-tellers and ice-cream vendors doing a roaring trade, trinket-stalls every few yards, the smoke and smell of barbecues already pervading the streets and alleys. Suddenly there are church bells; mass is about to begin. Crowds press forward towards the west door, but the church is already well-nigh filled to capacity. Yet more people try to press in, inching their way along the walls, standing on chairs and benches to obtain a better view. Once inside the church, the dark interior comes as a shock after the glare of morning sunlight in the square, and only the glimmer of hundreds of pilgrims' candles mounted on either side relieves the gloom of the ancient nave.

Suddenly there is the crackle of a microphone, and amid the shuffling and muttering of a packed congregation the priest's voice sounds above the murmur. A brief hush follows. Then, rising from the dark hollow of the nave the church is filled with the intoning of the responses—muffled words, uttered alternately in French and Provençal.

Finally the Magnificat. And as the music dies away a door in the ceiling high above the altar begins to open; in an instant the heads of the entire congregation tilt upwards as if a switch has been pressed. This is the moment everyone has been waiting for. From the small chapel concealed above the choir a painted chest, the shrine of the two Marys, is carefully, slowly, methodically lowered by cables. The entire church is now in silence except for the creaking of a pulley. It is one of those moments of well-orchestrated theatre at which the Catholic Church has always excelled. It is a moment when disbelief becomes willingly suspended for a short passage of unreal time as we gaze up and watch the shrine descending apparently from heaven in the midst of a church service. Once again we are witnessing the power and the drama of myth.

Then the silence ends. Voices break into a special hymn—*The Saints of Provence*. And cutting through the words of the hymn are spontaneous cries throughout the church: "Vivent les saintes!" and "Vive Sara!" because the time has come for the gypsy "saint" to join in the celebrations, and for her effigy to be carried up from the crypt to join the others. The moment of theatre is over: now comes the formal procession. This is the symbolic journey which takes these figures ceremonially back to the sea from where they came, and which in the minds of everyone who has ever come here and witnessed it represents the very heart of the folklore and magic of the Camargue.

Outside the church the slow procession has begun. Horses lead the way through the narrow streets of the town. These are the celebrated white horses of the Camargue, about which there will be much more to say, and they are ridden by the *gardians* who daily tend them and ride them as they round up the black bulls. All the horsemen are dressed now in their traditional clothing of moleskin trousers, coloured shirt, dark waistcoat and broad-brimmed hat, and they carry over their shoulders a long pole tipped with a metal trident in honour of Poseidon, the Greek god of the sea. Then, following the white horses comes the main body of the procession traditionally led by the Archbishop of Aix. Behind him bearers carry the effigies of the two Marys, who are raised high above the jostling crowds on a painted model of the Boat of Bethany. And next to them, born by gypsies on their shoulders, the statue of Sara, now robed in a cloud of white lace, is preceded by a banner portraying her goddess-like against a golden sky.

The ceremony is about to reach its climax—the blessing of the sea. The procession approaches the shore, and at this point the *gardians* on their white horses form a protective semi-circle with the water lapping against the animals' thighs while they stand facing the approaching bearers. Then slowly, step by step, they advance into the shallows, before very carefully lowering the effigies until, in an informal gesture of baptism, sea-water is gently sprinkled over them. Finally, having

received the benediction of the sea, the three effigies are carried back up the beach towards the town, accompanied by cries from the thousands who have been crowding around them on the shore—in Provençal now—*Salu! Salu! Viva les saintes! Viva Sara!*

The saints have made their annual return to the sea.

Now it is time for the final scene of this drama, as torches are raised to escort the effigies ceremonially back through the packed streets towards their fortress of a church which guards them and which, symbolically at least, they first built.

So the play is over for another year. And as the curtain falls the day of the Marys and of Sara takes on a different colour, exploding into fiesta, fireworks and song, until the sounds of celebration spread out across the lagoons and marshes of the Camargue, and the bars of the little town of Les Saintes-Maries-de-la-Mer overflow with the benediction of wine.

Chapter Three

VAN GOGH AND MISTRAL:
DREAMS OF PARADISE

Celebrated today as one of Europe's great wildernesses, the Camargue did not always enjoy a good press. One of the early complaints came from a disgruntled Archbishop of Arles in the seventeenth century who would clearly have preferred the area not to fall within his diocese. "The island [as it was frequently described] has a kind of heat that leads to despair four or five months of the year. There are mosquitoes, and... for three or four weeks in the summer there are flies in their thousands and millions which lead to desperation. They bite all the time."

Any visitor to the Camargue in high summer today is likely to share the archbishop's despair at the biting creatures which seem to be everywhere. The insects he describes as "flies" are known locally as *arabies*, and they do indeed bite all the time, though only for a brief period coinciding—whether by coincidence or design is unclear—with the flowering of the tamarisk bushes, usually in June. Mosquitoes, on the other hand, pervade the whole delta from early June until September. One of the more useless pieces of information available to visitors is that only the female mosquito carries a sting. Maybe tourists with twenty-twenty vision can spot the difference.

Bad reports continued to condemn the Camargue. In the year 1806 a businessman from Arles visiting Les Saintes-Marie-de-la-Mer described the town and its inhabitants in uncompromising language. He wrote of "vast cesspools out of which comes the ceaseless odour of pestilential vapours [which] makes staying here quite intolerable, and even those who live here often fall victim to diseases... Their character is gross and brutal; and their manners, since the Revolution, are very bad."

In spite of such unfavourable notices the nineteenth century in general brought a new and more appreciative audience to the Camargue, and with it a new sense of the romance of the place. The very qualities that had made previous generations shudder now appeared attractive. Wildernesses had come into fashion. The writings of Jean-Jacques Rousseau, and the Romantic movement in general, awakened the sensibilities of writers and painters to the delights of nature in the raw, as well as a curiosity towards whatever myths, legends and strange customs might be attached to unspoiled places. To be primitive was in some ill-defined way seen to be in touch with the pure wellsprings of life. Civilization was no longer the prerogative of those who dwelt in cities, Paris above all. Artists and writers were suddenly eager to move out into the wild, savouring the beauties of nature and the rustic charms of life in its midst. The countryside was where ones eyes could be opened to a way of life untainted by the rapacity, stress and corruption of the metropolis. Nature was where one could be cleansed and healed. It offered peace of mind and nourishment for the spirit. Here was a world which had managed to survive much as God intended it to be. It even bore the imprint of paradise itself. And if paradise was sometimes crude, mysterious and even hostile, then this was all the better for the human soul.

Such was the new Camargue as perceived by new Romantic eyes. In May 1888, three days after the annual festival of Sara and the

Marys, a young painter who had been living in Arles and revelling in the beauty of the Provençal countryside expressed his determination to travel to Les Saintes-Maries-de-la-Mer. His curiosity had been aroused by stories of the gypsies who regularly gathered there, and he was anxious to see the place for himself. In Arles he would have been well aware of these colourful travellers who regularly made their way up from Spain in their painted caravans. Besides, the legend of the Three Marys intrigued him—the notion of a vessel having once brought friends and relatives of Jesus to these far shores to begin the conversion of Provence to Christianity. He was himself a deeply religious man, having trained to become a pastor in his youth, both in his native Holland and in England.

The painter was, of course, Vincent Van Gogh. And on 28 May of that year he wrote to his brother Theo in Paris: "I expect to make an excursion to Saintes-Maries and see the Mediterranean at last."

This was a dream especially close to Van Gogh's heart. Unlike the cold, stormy North Sea he had known in Holland the Mediterranean symbolized everything to do with the south which he had travelled to discover and to record; it was a warm and benign sea beneath a sun which bathed the southern landscape in a brilliant kaleidoscope of colours. It was also where Van Gogh dreamed of founding a school of painting, and where he was soon to persuade Gauguin to join him— fatefully as it transpired. Meanwhile he was exploring this new world of colour and sunshine. He was like a pilgrim travelling purposefully from shrine to shrine.

"Early tomorrow I start for Saintes-Maries on the Mediterranean," he wrote excitedly to Theo on 29 May. 'I shall stay there till Saturday evening. I am taking two canvases, but I'm afraid it will probably be too windy to paint. You go by diligence. It is fifty kilometres from here. You cross the Camargue, grassy plains where there are herds of fighting bulls and also herds of little white horses, half wild and very beautiful."

At seven in the morning on Wednesday 30 May, Van Gogh left Arles by the regular horse-drawn diligence. (His painting of a brightly-coloured diligence similar to the one he travelled in survives.) The journey to Les Saintes-Maries, which was then little more than a small fishing village, took five hours of jolting discomfort. But once there the painter stayed five days. The lodgings cost him four francs a day, though the landlord had originally asked for six francs, he told Theo to his satisfaction.

He worked at fever-pitch as he invariably did, and during that stay of five days produced seven half-page drawings of the village done with a reed-pen, as well as one full-page drawing of Les Saintes-Maries seen from across the vineyards, and another of fishing-boats at sea with their tall curving sails—a study which he later used to create the background of one of his best-loved paintings, *Boats on the Beach at Saintes Maries*, now in the Van Gogh Museum in Amsterdam, and reproduced on a million-and-one calendars and postcards. It is a painting which has become an icon of the Camargue.

But it is his sketches of the old fishermen's houses which are the most vivid record of his stay in Les Saintes-Maries. They are drawn with the breathless energy of a man hungry to make use of every moment of the few days available to him there. "I do not believe there can be a hundred houses in the village," he wrote. He was specially drawn to the rows of reed-thatched cottages which at this time still made up much of the village, and which reminded him, he said, of those back home on the heaths and peat-bogs at Drenthe. Since these and other traditional Camargue houses have for the most part disappeared except for a scattering of them in the remoter marshlands, Van Gogh's loving record is an invaluable witness to what a Camargue village would have looked like before concrete and tourism took over.

In addition to the reed-thatched cottages he became obsessed with the colours of everything he set eyes on. Two months earlier, soon after his arrival in Arles, he had written excitedly to Theo: "I wanted to achieve colours like those in stained-glass windows." The subject on that occasion had been the little wooden drawbridge (or bascule bridge) he had discovered which crossed the canal running south from Arles, and which would have reminded him nostalgically of his native Holland. Van Gogh's much-loved paintings of the bridge survive, though the bridge itself was pulled down in 1935—replaced today by a faithful replica ironically described on the map as the "Pont Van Gogh".

Van Gogh took with him his excitement at the colours of the south wherever he travelled in Provence; and during his five days in Les Saintes-Maries he found plenty of material to feed that excitement. "One night I went for a walk by the sea along the empty shore," he wrote to his brother. "It was not exactly lively, but neither was it sad: it was—beautiful! The deep-blue sky was flecked with clouds of a blue deeper than the blue of intense cobalt... And in the blue depth the stars were sparkling, greenish, yellow, white, rose, flashing more like jewels than they do at home—even in Paris: opals you might call them, emeralds, lapis, rubies, sapphires."

At the same time, colours were not quite everything to Van Gogh. "You get better fried fish here than on the Seine," he assured Theo.

Thirty-three years before Van Gogh made his journey across the Camargue to Les Saintes-Maries a young poet from Avignon fulfilled a similar desire to see the place of pilgrimage for himself. He was little known at the time, but his journey was to supply the crucial ingredient of an epic romance, written in the native Provençal language, which was shortly to win him the accolade among his peers of "the Provençal Dante" and even "the Homer of Provence". The poem made him the universally acknowledged champion of a Provençal literary revival, and many years later contributed more than anything else he ever wrote to the award of the Nobel Prize for Literature in 1904. The epic poem was *Mirèio*, or in French *Mireille*. And its author, soon to become a household name throughout France, was Frédéric Mistral.

The journey which began it all was one that Mistral recounted in his memoirs, *Mei Origins*. "All my life I had heard of the Camargue and of Les Saintes Maries and the pilgrimage to that shrine, but I had never yet been there." So, a little after midnight on 24 May 1855, the day of the festival of the Two Marys, he and a writer friend called Mathieu met in the town of Beaucaire, south of Avignon, and mounted a diligence along with a company of men, women and children. There may have been more than one diligence since no fewer than fourteen passengers made the journey (not counting the chickens), and these were "packed into wagons as tight as sardines in a tin"—so tight, Mistral explained, that one passenger had to be seated on the shafts of the vehicle with his legs dangling.

Any discomfort of the journey was amply relieved, however, by the presence of a young girl seated right behind Mistral: "a more beautiful sight than the rising sun... as she emerged all smiling and fresh like a goddess of youth. A dark red ribbon caught up her blonde hair." Mistral then gets into his literary stride as he describes her lips, her skin and in particular her smile, which was "like a flower shaking off the morning dew." What especially appealed to the romantic in Mistral was that the girl, whose name he discovered was Alarde, was actually suffering from a broken heart, and was travelling to Les Saintes-Maries in the forlorn hope of meeting her husband-to-be who had deserted her for another woman. (How such a tragic state of mind could tally with a smile like a flower shaking off the morning dew Mistral omits to explain.) He was by now entirely captivated, while all the time he was lost in adoration the diligence "struggled slowly through the vast plains of the Camargue."

To add to the hazards of the journey a ferocious storm then burst over the marshes, flooding the road and making further progress impossible. The passengers were compelled to complete their journey on foot; and here the gallant poet became the hero of the hour by lifting the beautiful Alarde in his arms and carrying her to safety through the swirling waters. "Her hair brushed against mine," Mistral explained breathlessly; yet all the time he was carrying her, he realized sadly, all the girl could think about was her lost lover.

How long he actually carried her we are not told: only that the long night eventually ended and dawn broke over a bleak Camargue. And finally the bedraggled party arrived at Les Saintes-Maries.

Mistral's account of his dramatic journey was written many decades after the event, and how much of it matches what actually took place on that stormy night in May 1855 we shall never know. His travelling companion and fellow-poet, Mathieu, perhaps out of loyalty to his friend, never seems to have commented on the incident, even though he must have witnessed whatever took place. Maybe there is a code of solidarity among poets. In any case the truth or otherwise of the story is beside the point. More valuable is the poetic coincidence by which Mistral and the girl are described as arriving at the church of Les Saintes-Maries just in time to observe the ceremony of the shrine of the Two Marys being lowered from the small chapel above the high altar. What follows is among the earliest and most vivid eye-witness account of the dramatic moment which is at the very heart of the annual celebrations of the two saints from the sea.

Mistral describes the smell of the burning tapers within the church, the suffocating heat, the deafening sound of each group of pilgrims "singing their own particular canticle at the top of their voices... until, high above us, the shrines begin to descend, and the crowd bursts into shouts and cries of 'Oh Great Saints Mary'." At this very moment, Mistral explains, the beautiful Alarde appeared, rushing distraught down the length of the nave towards the altar pleading desperately to the saints to give her back her lover.

It is heady stuff! In his memoirs Mistral pursues the heart-rending story of Alarde no further. Perhaps it had no further to go, or else fiction had already taken over. What he had witnessed in his dramatic journey to the Camargue was to become the core of the epic romance which we know he had already begun. The storm and the distraught heroine may have arrived at exactly the right moment. Alarde was soon to become Mirèio, and Mistral awarded her an extra touch of tragedy by making the pursuit of her lover end in suicide.

In his memoirs Mistral offers no such agonizing dramatics. The account of his actual journey to Les Saintes-Maries ends on a wistful note. The following day he watches the procession of the saints to the sea-shore: "Looking out over the wide glistening sea... illuminated by radiant sunshine, it seemed to us that we were on the threshold of Paradise." And the sea, of course, reminds him of the legend from which this place was born. In *Mirèio*, he comes to recount that legend in verse: *Sus uno ratamalo, I furour de la mar/E sènso velo e sènso ramo,/Fugueriaembardi* ("In the raging sea they were cruelly driven/In a ship without a sail/Without an oar.")

Mistral's *Mirèio* is a paean to the Camargue. He writes of it as "an immense plain/a wilderness stretching beyond sight/further and further." But it is also a threatening and desolate place, a mirror of the darkness of the human soul and a setting for strife and drama, much as another author of the High Romantic era, Thomas Hardy, chose to depict Egdon Heath. Mistral's tale pulls together the Christian myth of the Camargue, its bleak landscape, the way of life which is alternately uncouth and idyllic, and makes it the perfect setting for a tragic love-story. His heroine, just like the beautiful Alarde whom he once carried through the swirling floodwaters, is a young girl who makes a desperate pilgrimage to seek the help of the saints in Les Saintes-Maries to reunite her with her beloved. But unlike Alarde, Mirèio takes her own life in the crypt of the church, dying in the arms of her parents and the lover who had betrayed her.

Mistral completed *Mirèio* in 1859. The most celebrated French poet of his day, Alphonse de Lamartine, declared when he read it: "This is Homer!" A more appropriate comparison might have been: "This is Byron!" The two poets were barely two generations apart and shared a taste for the melodramatizing of history and legend in resounding verse. "Le Grand Byron", as the French had come to call him, would certainly have been familiar to Mistral, at least in translation; indeed, *Mirèio* is a story which Lord Byron himself might well have invented.

The fame of *Mirèio*, especially when translated into French as *Mireille*, was not unlike that enjoyed by Byron, and it certainly helped propel the Camargue into celebrity. Gounod adapted Mistral's poem as the libretto for his opera of the same name, and it was duly performed in the Roman arena at Arles in the august presence of Mistral himself. Then in 1904 came the award of the Nobel Prize for Literature (actually a shared award that year). And even though Mistral's literary output had been prolific over the previous forty-five years it was for *Mirèio* that the author was still chiefly renowned. Among his world-wide admirers was the American president Theodore Roosevelt who wrote to Mistral when the prize was announced, claiming proudly that he had owned a copy of the book for twenty years. He went on to voice his opinion on material success—which he had no wish to undervalue, he assured the poet—yet, he went on, "I only desire that they shall never make us forget that besides the nation's body there is also the nation's soul."

No sentiments could have been closer to Mistral's heart. He could have asked for nothing more valuable than to be able to reach the nation's soul—the nation in question, of course, being Provence, and certainly not France.

The poet's fame across the Atlantic was not confined to America's president. When Colonel William Cody brought his troop of Wild West performers to Europe, "Buffalo Bill", as he described himself, was delighted to take his cowboys south to Provence to perform before the great man in a region where wild horses and black bulls roamed the landscape, and therefore where he could feel at home. The two men became close friends. Buffalo Bill even left Mistral his brace of pistols when he departed, still on display in Arles in the Musée Arlaten. Cody also gave him a dog, a present which the poet deeply cherished as a memento of his friend from the Wild West. A portrait of a dog, presumably the same one, is to be seen on Mistral's tomb in the village of Maillane, on the edge of the Alpilles hills, where he lived for much of his life.

Finally in 1920, six years after the poet's death, that youthful journey to the Camargue which had given birth to his tragic theme was commemorated in the form of a life-size bronze statue of Mireille (Mirèio) placed near the ancient church at Les Saintes-Maries-de-la-Mer, where in the author's mind the drama of her young life had reached its bitter climax. Here on her lofty plinth Mistral's heroine stands, gesticulating agonizingly towards the cruel world which had betrayed her.

⁓

Provence has never quite recovered from Frédéric Mistral. He remains the region's prophet just as his *Mirèio* is its talisman. The Museum of the Camargue even devotes a substantial section to "the Camargue at the time of Mireille", as though his tragic heroine personified all that was most authentic and meaningful about the region, and as if she was the Camargue's dark soul. Mistral remains one of those mythical presences who are impossible to ignore—perhaps less as a reality than as an idea. He haunts the consciousness of those of us who ask "What is special about Provence? What makes it different?" For Mistral that "specialness" lay in the persistence of a vibrant culture of the south which had long been buried under an oppressive French dominance controlled by Paris, and which it was his single-minded ambition to revive. And the means of that revival was, for him, language: in other words a revival of *langue d'oc*, the native language of the south which had also been the language of the troubadour poets and of Good King Réné's "court of the sun", but which had been systematically crushed by the French language of the north, *langue d'oil*.

Mistral's vision was of an ancient nation destined to be reborn through the power of words. It would be a nation possessed with the gift of tongues, no longer tyrannized and tongue-tied by Paris. Essentially it was a poet's vision, because it was in the medium of poetry that language had always found its purest voice, and thence its power to enlighten the minds of those who listened. Poets were invested with a mystic importance. They were seers. They were prophets. They held a golden key to Paradise. In Provence to this day poets tend to be held in special awe, as almost a race apart, a respect which is a reflection of the aura they carry rather than of the number of books they may sell.

Such at any rate was Mistral's lifelong crusade; it was the pursuit of national identity, and therefore collective status and pride, through language. He resolved, he declared, "to restore the natural and traditional

The distraught Mireille, Les Saintes-Maries.

language of this land." Nationalism and literary ambition marched heroically hand in hand.

In his memoirs he wrote: "It had always aggravated me to find that our language was used only in derision." That aggravation would have been particularly sore since his mother apparently spoke only Provençal. She was a village girl, the daughter of the local mayor who had married a patrician figure almost twice her age. Mistral's father had first set eyes on her as she was gathering corn in the fields, as though she had stepped out of a painting by Millet, and in the appropriate romantic manner of the times he had fallen instantly in love with her before they even exchanged a word. They settled in her native village of Maillane, to the east of Arles. Frédéric was their first child. He was born on 8 September 1830, and narrowly escaped being named Nostradamus after the celebrated physician and astrologer who was supposed once to have lived in the village. However, convention prevailed (as well as perhaps consideration for the poor boy) and Frédéric he became.

As a student in Avignon his teacher was a poet by the name of Joseph Roumanille. Mistral recorded how Roumanille was passionate about restoring the written language of Provençal, *langue d'oc*, or *Occitan*, insisting that it be composed "in the old style as employed by the ancient troubadours." Mistral was an enthusiastic convert to the cause, and together the two men, along with a handful of eager recruits, founded a literary society in Avignon which they called the Félibrige, a name derived apparently from an obscure religious ditty which Mistral had heard sung in his native village of Maillane; it meant "doctor" or "sage".

The year was 1854, and the newly-formed band of sages duly set out with missionary zeal "to renew the skin of our language."

Mistral himself was now twenty-four. He had already started work on the epic poem *Mirèio*, which was soon to become the flagship of the Félibrige. It was also just a single year before he made his epic trek across the Camargue to Les Saintes-Maries, a journey which was to provide him with the poem's tragic denouement. His companion on that journey, Anselme Mathieu, had become another early recruit to the Félibrige fraternity.

After *Mirèio* Mistral's literary activities were profuse and varied. His first commitment was to devote twelve years to compiling a dictionary of the Provençal language in seven dialects. For a creative writer in the prime of youth to devote more than a decade to so dogged an endeavour is proof enough of his commitment to the Provençal cause. Yet here also lay one of the snags attending the whole Félibrige crusade: *langue d'oc*, as they employed it in their poetry, may indeed have been the tongue of the troubadours and of the poets who made up the glittering court of Good King Réné. It was not, however, the living language of the street but of a series of aristocratic courts which had long ago disappeared. What was still spoken in the more remote towns and villages of the south varied considerably from place to place. Being a spoken language used for the most part by barely-literate peasants, it had never been systematized or given any kind of uniformity. The only *lingua franca*—common at least to the more educated classes—had been French, the language of the "conquerors". The Provençal language, on the other hand, was little more than a hotchpotch of local variations which had much in common as well as a great deal that was not in common. What Mistral and the Félibrige strove to establish was at best a kind of linguistic omelette whisked together from ingredients plucked from widely-varying locations and cultures: hence Mistral's dictionary in seven dialects. There might well have been a lot more than seven.

As a spoken tongue, at least Provençal was an authentic living language, however varied it might be from place to place. It was hardly the language of the troubadours which the Félibrige yearned for, but it was how ordinary people communicated within their own communities. Yet this too was under threat, not from worthy attempts at standardization, but from Parisian tyranny. The reaction of the French cultural moguls to Mistral's crusade was to intensify pressure on local authorities in the south to outlaw the speaking of Provençal in school, even to the extent of encouraging the punishment of children who disobeyed.

Mistral, not surprisingly, was outraged.

A curious, and curiously moving, testimony to the poet's crusade is the museum he established in the heart of Arles, the ancient Roman city which is one of the gateways to the Camargue and where Mistral spent much of the latter part of his life. In 1896, when he was in his late sixties, he conceived another of his hugely ambitious plans, which was to create a "true museum of the life and people of the region". He began to collect artefacts of all kinds—household utensils, farming equipment, furniture, pottery, domestic implements and knick-knacks, photographs, documents, examples of local costume (a particular obsession of his)—in fact anything that demonstrated the traditional way of life of local people. Mistral wanted to bring all these objects together "before the ignorance of pretended progress had wiped them out," he announced trenchantly.

Museums of traditional country life have become commonplace in our own times, the Museum of the Camargue in the Mas du Pont de Rousty, opened in 1979, being an attractive local example But in the late nineteenth century the idea was novel, and doubtless considered at the time to be somewhat quaint. Who among the Provençal bourgeoisie in the early 1900s would have considered it of the slightest value to celebrate the lifestyle of peasants? For Mistral, however, the idea was anything but quaint, and certainly not an exercise in sentimental nostalgia. Quite the opposite: to him the objects on display represented timeless values which he was convinced would ultimately prevail over the false ones currently thrown up by the urban industrialized world. Then, in 1904, he was awarded the Nobel Prize, and with the prize-money he was able to purchase a sixteenth-century mansion in the centre of the city, the Hôtel de Castellane-Laval, to house his growing collection. This became the Musée Arlaten, about which he wrote triumphantly: "the museum's collections will become life-buoys serving as the guide for a future renaissance."

In life, as in language, the past for Mistral was the way forward.

The thirty-three rooms of the Musée (Museon in Provençal) Arlaten inevitably have a somewhat fusty look today—a blend of ethnographical collection and Old Curiosity Shop. There are areas devoted to Mistral's writings and to those of the Félibrige. One room contains souvenirs of the writer Alphonse Daudet (who lived not far away in his famous windmill near the Alpilles) and his close friendship with Mistral. In fact Daudet was not an unqualified admirer of Mistral's world. Inspired by the poet, and doubtless by having read *Mireille*, he paid a dutiful visit to the Camargue. Whatever he may have reported to Mistral himself about the experience, in letters to other friends he made his feelings extremely clear. He wrote of "the dreary monotony of the place... unfit for human habitation", and went on to comment on the deadly menace of fever. It was one thing to live in a windmill, quite another to live in a malarial swamp.

A further room in the museum is devoted to the history of the former kingdom of Arles, while another dwells on the various mythical monsters of the region. A good deal of space is given over to the founder's own passion for Arlesian costume, with designs for appropriate dresses including examples of painful-looking corsets and portraits of grim ladies who are presumably wearing them. A further room celebrates one of Mistral's fondest inventions, the Festival of Virgins, over which he would preside annually in Arles' Roman theatre.

The beauty of the women of Arles was well acknowledged long before Mistral made a public celebration of it with his annual festival. None the less he certainly did much to spread the word abroad. One man who was travelling through Provence at the time when Mistral was staging his Festival of Virgins was the formidable Victorian writer and journalist, Sir Theodore Andrea Cook. In the account of his travels, *Old Provence*, which was first published in the year Mistral was awarded the Nobel Prize, Cook noted with misty eyes that the young beauties of Arles "seem the immortal relics of a golden age that has, elsewhere, vanished from the earth."

A few years later, a more lusty visitor from Britain, the painter Augustus John, travelled to Arles from Martigues where he was living on the edge of the Camargue specially to enjoy the famed beauty of its women, later noting in his autobiography how delighted he had been that "on special occasions the young ones resume their ancestral garments."

John also wrote that he regularly caught sight of Mistral visiting his museum. In fact every Thursday over the last decade of his life Mistral would spend the entire day in his beloved Musée Arlaten, checking on displays and making certain that the female attendants were wearing the correct Arlesian costumes—a practice to which they adhere to this day. John never actually met Mistral, though he did write to ask him if he would be prepared to sit for his portrait. Mistral's reply was curt: *Jamais, monsieur! Jamais!*

Doubtless he had never heard of Augustus John. Even more certain is that he would never have heard of another painter who, two decades earlier, had set up his easel little more than a stone's-throw from Mistral's museum-to-be in order to record the city's café life by night in the Place du Forum. It is an engaging thought that Mistral might easily have passed by one September evening in 1888 when the artist was painting the *Terrasse de Café la Nuit*. And had he paused to take some interest in the brightly-coloured canvas and engaged the artist in lively conversation, then instead of the stuffy likenesses of Mistral which peer down at us from the museum walls, the Musée Arlaten might now be displaying a portrait masterpiece by Van Gogh.

But that is another lost dream.

Chapter Four

ARLES AND ST.-GILLES:
ENTRANCES AND EXITS

The Camargue has two gateways. The Roman city of Arles is one of them. The pilgrimage town of St.-Gilles is the other, further to the west. Each possesses a magnificent medieval church, dedicated to a local saint. Both have been much revered and have inspired many miracles, though like many early Christian saints, each is of somewhat dubious historical origin. St. Trophimus (St. Trophime) may or may not have been the first bishop of Arles in the third century, or possibly earlier, even though Roman Gaul was not officially Christian until at least a century later. As for St. Gilles, his origins are even more complex, and will be treated later in this chapter. Meanwhile, let us consider St. Trophime, and the great church which is dedicated to him.

Among many legends attached to the saint was the belief that he was buried in the Roman necropolis on the edge of the city known as Les Alyscamps (meaning Elysian Fields). The site was Christianized at the time of the Emperor Constantine early in the fourth century, after which it became transformed into one of the most romantic burial-grounds in the Christian world—which it still is. This was partly due to its location. Until relatively recent times, Les Alyscamps acted as the principal means of approaching the city, inviting the visitor to process (like the Appian Way on the edge of Rome) along a grandiose corridor flanked by tombs, chapels and mausoleums dedicated to the noble dead. To enter Arles this way was to be made to feel in awe; here was no ordinary city, but the capital of a large section of a former empire, and hence comparable to no less a city than Rome itself.

Over the centuries Les Alyscamps has attracted scores of impressionable visitors, including writers and painters, the most famous in more recent times being Gauguin and Van Gogh, both of whom painted the place during the brief tempestuous period when they shared the little yellow house in Arles.

The present church of St.-Trophime, in the centre of Arles, dates from the late eleventh and twelfth centuries, its various predecessors having been comprehensively wrecked by barbarian invaders from the north and finally by Saracens from the south during the eighth century. The church is a majestic product of what has been called "the twelfth-century Renaissance", a time of relative stability and prosperity in western Europe when Christian institutions flourished. In the words of the Cluniac monk and chronicler Raoul Glaber, "one would have thought that the world itself was casting aside its old age and clothing itself anew in a white mantle of churches."

In 1152 what was believed to be the body of St. Trophimus was joyfully brought from Les Alyscamps to be re-buried at the site of the new church now well under construction. Two and a half decades later the nave was sufficiently completed for the Holy Roman Emperor Barbarossa to be crowned there. And in 1190 the building was brought to a glorious completion in the form of one of the finest carved portals in southern France. It opens on to the main square of the city, known inevitably today as the Place de la République, though the city's classical past is handsomely acknowledged in the shape of a Roman obelisk placed in the centre of the square. But then the spirit of Ancient Rome is everywhere in this city; wherever you walk, wherever you look, Caesar's ghost haunts the place. Even the great carved portal of St.-Trophime itself makes an acknowledgment to that classical past, the semi-circular shape surmounting the tympanum above the door giving a distinct echo of a Roman triumphal arch.

The ranks of sculpture above and on either side of the main door illustrate a theme which is repeated thousands of times on Romanesque churches of this period: Christ in Majesty. This was a moment in European history when Christianity was reasserting its moral authority as well as its power over people's minds after the anarchy of the Dark Ages. Right over the entrance, in the centre of the tympanum, sits Christ as the Supreme Judge, while around him are arranged the symbols of the four evangelists whose gospels will spread His word far and wide. For the benefit of any remaining doubters the theme of Divine Judgment is rammed home by the customary scenes of the Last Judgment; and these are complemented by further scenes illustrating the sufferings of early Christian martyrs, all executed with the customary ghoulish relish. Van Gogh, for one, found the stoning of Stephen "so cruel, so monstrous" that it seemed to him "to belong to another world, and I am glad not to belong to it"—sentiments probably shared even by those who have grown accustomed to the punitive vision of the medieval church. But then, how often do we find ourselves admiring the architecture and artistry of Raoul Glaber's "white mantle of churches", and yet recoiling from the relentlessly dark sermons in stone which decorate them!

Passing through those grandiloquent doors to the interior of St.-Trophime, it is suddenly a dark and sombre place, like so many Romanesque churches before Gothic windows let in the light. This is somewhere to pray and to feel somewhat crushed by the weight of stone and the weight of divine authority. But then, outside again, to the right of the church, the mood changes once more. Here, hidden away in the very heart of the city, are the loveliest cloisters in Provence, bathed in southern sunlight, two of the galleries Romanesque, two of them

Gothic built two centuries later. Unusually these cloisters were never attached to a monastery, but were designed to be a place where the canons could meet at a time when St.-Trophime had the status of a cathedral. The difference between the two functions, that of church and of the cloisters, translates into the feel of each place. The church was for silent prayer and ritual plainsong, whereas the cloister was a meeting-place for talk and a sharing of thoughts.

Dominating both the church and cloisters of St. Trophime, and rising above the ancient city like a finger pointing to heaven, is the majestic twelfth-century bell-tower, the finest in Provence, and visible for miles. From the highest gallery of the tower the Camargue fans out across those hundreds of square miles all the way southwards to the sea. If the church of St.-Trophime were still a cathedral, the Camargue would be its diocese.

From Arles a road heads directly westwards, crossing the Grand Rhône just outside the city to enter what is still described as the "island" of the Camargue. It circuits the flooded rice-fields and the rich pastures where the famous black bulls raise their heads to glower as you pass. Then, after eight miles or so, the road crosses the second branch of the river, the Petit Rhône, and after a short distance reaches a town which has long been the second gateway to the Camargue: St.-Gilles.

In any hall of fame St.-Gilles can claim as great a prominence as Arles, for two distinctive reasons. In the Middle Ages the town was one of the leading pilgrimage centres in western Europe, chiefly on account of its association with the pilgrim route to Santiago de Compostela in north-west Spain.

By contrast, the town of St.-Gilles was also the scene of an event that sparked a war of horrific savagery which effectively put an end to the political independence of Languedoc. The war was known as the Albigensian Crusade, an opportunist exercise sponsored by the French king and the papacy in Rome, and mounted against the heretical

Cathars of Languedoc, the crusade being named after the city of Albi, one of the Cathars' principal strongholds.

But before dwelling on that bloodstained moment of history there is a brighter chapter in the story of St.-Gilles, in the shape of another of those legends in which the Camargue abounds. The identity of early Christian saints being invariably lost in mists of myth, we have no more than a hazy image of the man who gave his name to this town. Legend has it that Gilles was born in Greece early in the seventh century, and that by divine calling he chose to set out on a raft which brought him in due course to the shores of Provence, no doubt assisted by the same benevolent currents that had brought the Three Marys and black Sara to these shores seven centuries earlier. Here Gilles lived the life of a Christian hermit in a cave, befriended, so the story goes, by a doe he had miraculously saved by intercepting a huntsman's javelin. The doe in gratitude proceeded to bring the hermit regular supplies of food. The huntsman, astonished by the miracle he had witnessed, turned out to be king of the Visigothic tribe which had recently conquered the area, and being a wealthy man as well as a convert to Christianity he undertook to found an abbey on the site, of which Gilles became the first abbot.

So much for legend. The earliest historical references to the abbey date from two centuries later. They make it clear that St.-Gilles was by this time much revered and much visited by popes and other church and civic dignitaries, Gilles himself having by this time been duly canonized by one of those visiting popes. Then, during the latter part of the eleventh century the cult of St. Gilles expanded to a bewildering degree, primarily because the abbey had been drawn into the net cast by the great Benedictine abbey of Cluny, in southern Burgundy. Cluny was the fountain of monastic reform at the time. Life in monasteries had become generally slack and—in many eyes—distinctly ungodly, certainly far from the humble and dedicated vocation proclaimed as the model of how a servant of Christ should live by the founder of the Benedictine Order, St. Benedict, five centuries earlier. St.-Gilles was one of a large number of abbeys, many of them located in Languedoc

or in neighbouring regions, which had become placed under the benevolent authority of Cluny in order that they should undergo much-
needed reforms. These included strict adherence to the disciplines laid
down in the Rule of St. Benedict, composed in the sixth century by
Benedict himself, and originally intended for the benefit of the
monastery he had found at Monte Cassino, in southern Italy.

The man largely responsible for this expansion of Cluniac power
and influence was the most outstanding of all Cluny's abbot, Hugh the
Great, a feudal aristocrat of remarkable gifts who presided over the
abbey of Cluny and its expanding empire for sixty years until his death
in the year 1109.

Abbot Hugh was a man of massive political as well as spiritual authority. He was a friend and adviser of popes, emperors and kings, including William the Conqueror, as well as possessing a great many
passionately held ambitions. One of Hugh's most urgent missions was
to push back the forces of Islam from Spain and so reclaim the Iberian
Peninsula for Christianity. Accordingly it was here, at the gateway of the
Camargue, that the abbey of St.-Gilles came to be one of the key players
in such a venture, contributing to an unlikely partnership between
monastic life and military conquest.

How and why this partnership occurred was due to that phenomenon of the early Middle Ages, the pilgrimage movement, and in
particular the most popular pilgrimage of the age, to the shrine of St.
James the apostle and cousin of Christ at Santiago de Compostela in
north-west Spain. It is estimated that by the eleventh century more
than half a million pilgrims trod the roads to Santiago every year. And
numbers continued at this level for several hundred years; early in the
fourteenth century the poet Dante declared that so many people took
to the pilgrim road that its course could be traced in the stars in the
form of the Milky War. For pilgrims it was the long road to heaven, a
means of obtaining absolution, *remission peccatorum*, remission of a
person's sins. People went on pilgrimage as a form of penance, as a
punishment for a crime they had committed, as well as for a variety of
more or less adventurous reasons. The route across northern Spain had

only recently been freed from Saracen control, which certainly increased its appeal, and the part played by Cluny in establishing a network of abbeys and priories along the route was a vital contribution to the security of the region. They acted as service stations for travellers, offering a safe house, a bed for the night, a meal, a psalm, a prayer, companionship, even medical help. The poor gave thanks in return, while the rich gave money in the form of donations and endowments. In cooperation with grateful Spanish rulers, roads and bridges were built, towns fortified, trade increased, and the local population began at last to feel relatively safe.

As a result the Christian hold on northern Spain became immeasurably strengthened. Politics and pilgrimages advanced hand in hand, and under the patronage of Cluny the roads the pilgrims took became perfect conduits for Christian expansion. They threaded their way across the French countryside like a giant spider's web, merging eventually into a single principal road on the southern side of the Pyrenees, in Navarre, before striking westwards towards Galicia and distant Santiago close to the Atlantic and the end of the known world: Cape Finisterre, as it is still called.

St.-Gilles occupied a key place in this network of pilgrim roads, as we know from a remarkable document which has come down to us. A few decades after the abbey became a dependency of Cluny a man by the name of Aimery Picaud, a Cluniac monk from the Poitou region of Aquitaine, was responsible (or at least he is the most likely candidate) for putting together a manuscript in Latin known as the *Codex Calixtinus* or *Liber sancti Jacobi*, the Book of St. James. It is a compilation of five books, the fifth being a pilgrims' guide for travellers to Santiago, which can reasonably lay claim to be the first-ever tourist guide-book. Picaud is known to have made the journey himself in the company of a lady called Ginberga, who later donated a manuscript of the *Codex* (very possibly the original) to the cathedral of Santiago, where it remains to this day as the cathedral library's most prized possession. The guide consists of a graphic account of what we can assume to have been the author's own journey across France and northern Spain, divided into a series of stages and describing what pilgrims might expect to find were they to follow in his footsteps. It is packed with juicy local gossip and a wealth of unashamed prejudice about everything that meets the author's disapproval, from murderous boatmen to uncouth peasantry. It exists in translation and makes colourful reading—like a Rough Guide to medieval France and Spain.

Picaud explains that there were four main pilgrim routes in France which converged on northern Spain and became a single road heading west. One of these roads began in Paris, the second in Vézélay in northern Burgundy, the third in Le Puy on the eastern edge of the Auvergne—while the fourth and most southerly of the four roads began at the abbey of St.-Gilles.

Here, in Aimery Picaud's eyes, lay the supreme importance of the abbey, and his comments spell it out. "It is necessary," he writes, "to pay the most respectful visit to the venerable relics of Saint Gilles, pious confessor and abbot, because Saint Gilles, famous throughout the world, should be venerated and loved by everyone. After the prophets and the apostles no one is more worthy than he, nor more holy, more bathed in glory, or more ready to come to man's aid."

With those credentials it is no wonder that the fame of the place spread throughout the Christian world. The prestige of the abbey of St.-Gilles in the twelfth century is perfectly reflected in the scale and grandeur of the abbey church—at least the area of it which has survived the ravages of history. Here is one of the most glorious church façades in Europe, and the supreme masterpiece of Romanesque art and architecture in Provence. The church itself was begun early in the century, the great façade spanning its entire width being created over the following forty years at much the same time as the portal of St.-Trophime in Arles, probably by sculptors and stonemasons from the same workshop. The whole ensemble is known to have been completed by the middle of the twelfth century. We also know the name of one of the principal sculptors responsible for it, because inscribed on the statue of St. Jude, between the northern and central portal is the legend BRUNUS ME FECIT, "Brunus made me." It is all we know about the man, which is none the less more than we know about most sculptors of the Middle Ages, even those responsible for some of the finest carvings in stone that have come down to us.

More than a touch of Roman grandeur enriches the abbey church of St.-Gilles. Set high above a flight of stone steps, its façade stretches majestically to the left and right as you gaze up at it—a blend of triumphal arch and bible story told in stone. It is made up of three elaborate portals side by side, each decorated with wonderfully lively, vigorous carvings that are set within ranks of Corinthian columns, and with a frieze of further figures illustrating the life of Christ and his disciples clustered between the portals. A tympanum crowns each portal. The central tympanum is devoted to the traditional theme of Christ in Glory, the northern one to the Virgin and the Nativity, while the theme of the Crucifixion dominates the south tympanum. Besides the wealth of carved figures, the sheer breadth of the façade adds an extra meaning to the building—an air of expansiveness and optimism. It is as if this complex ensemble of carvings and columns had been created quite deliberately in order to express the expanding ambitions of a renascent church which at this very moment in history was recruiting pilgrims and armed knights from all over France in the cause of a holy war against the Saracens in Spain, and which before long was to launch two crusades to the Holy Land under the leadership of the French king Louis IX from a port only a few miles from here (see Chapter 6).

This was a time of glory for St.-Gilles. It was a gateway not only to the Camargue but to the Holy Land as well as to Spain. In the years before Jerusalem fell to the forces of Islam in 1187 many pilgrims bravely setting out for the Bible lands departed from here (the port of Aigues-Mortes did not yet exist). At the same time, and in considerably greater numbers, those preparing to take the pilgrim road to Santiago de Compostela first congregated here in order to worship the legendary St. Gilles, whom Aymery Picaud described as "famous throughout the world".

Then storm-clouds appeared on the horizon. Scarcely more than half a century after the completion of the great abbey church an event took place in St.-Gilles which was to be the lightning-strike that would damage the fortunes of this entire region—politically and socially—as profoundly as any event in the long history of Languedoc and Provence. It was an act of murder—hardly a rare event in medieval church circles, it is true; yet even by the standards of the age this was a very special murder, one that in a short space of time ignited a sizeable area of Europe. It was to be the first major war within Christianity.

The story of that devastating storm, in brief, is this. The most powerful rulers of the region were the counts of Toulouse. They owned much of Languedoc and their home base was the town of St.-Gilles, where they had one of their numerous castles. Theirs was a highly prestigious and honoured dynasty. An earlier count, Raymond of St.-Gilles, had been among the most successful leaders of the First Crusade in 1095, in the course of which he had led a triumphant assault on Jerusalem in 1098. Over the following century the political ambitions of successive counts became ever more expansive, while their means of fulfilling them tended to veer between ruthlessness and deviousness. Pre-eminent among these ambitions seems to have been a grand design, perhaps more instinctive than clearly drawn, for the independence of a Greater Languedoc, in other words a region which would be free of the looming presence of the kings of France on the one hand, and of the papacy on the other—with, of course, the counts of Toulouse holding the principal reins of power.

This would appear to be the most likely motive behind the family's involvement in the events surrounding the St.-Gilles murder. The lords of Toulouse were not men who took kindly to being told what to do, none more stubbornly so than Raymond VI who became count of Toulouse in 1194. It was Raymond's ill-hidden ambitions which were to bring him inevitably, and disastrously, into conflict with France as well as with Rome. The flashpoint of their differences was the issue of religious heresy—or, more specifically, Raymond's unwillingness to take punitive action against the heretical Cathars whose stronghold was the very region of which he was the ruler, and with whom

The ornate façade of the abbey church of St.-Gilles.

Raymond not surprisingly had much sympathy, even if it was only because the Cathars were opposed to church orthodoxy and therefore deeply opposed to the authority of Rome. In Raymond's eyes they symbolized regional independence for Languedoc.

The Cathars were the most popular—and the most successful—heretical sect within Christianity until the emergence of Protestantism three centuries later, with which they had much in common, protesting as they did against the venality and corruption of the established church of the day, which they perceived to be an un-Christian tyranny in which God had become replaced by Mammon. The core of the Cathar faith was startlingly simple: it was a belief that the world was created not by God alone, but by God and the Devil, God having been responsible for all matters of the spirit, and the Devil for the material world. It followed that the only people free of the stain of Satan were those who renounced all pleasures of the flesh (even though they were themselves "of the flesh"—a contradiction hard to resolve). These Cathari elite were known as *perfecti*, or "perfects", and they were seen as the saviours of mankind on this earth—humble in a way priests of the orthodox church were seen not to be, unburdened as they were by riches and other worldly goods. At the same time the perfects were glad to offer a reprieve to the sons of Satan before their death in the form of what was called the *consolamentum*.

From the viewpoint of our own times this would seem a not-unreasonable set of beliefs given the terrors and superstitions of the age, and it is hard to understand why so benign and simplistic a doctrine should have aroused such passionate hated in orthodox Christian circles. The answer has to lie in the state of Christendom at the time. By the late twelfth century, particularly after the fall of Jerusalem to the Saracens in 1187, leaders of the church felt increasingly under threat from Islam. Accordingly they chose increasingly to cling to a rigid orthodoxy as a raft of safety; there could be no weak links in their own armour. Heresy was seen as the enemy within, and tolerance of any deviation from official dogma was a sign of weakness and vulnerability—to be crushed.

From his castle in St.-Gilles Count Raymond seems not to have seen it this way. It is unlikely that he cared about heresy one way or another. He was a political animal, anxious above all to preserve—and if possible to extend—his territories and his power. Accordingly, when urged by the pope to take action against the Cathars, he did what political animals invariably do when pressed to act against their will: he did nothing.

The response of Pope Innocent III was at first diplomatic. In 1203 he replaced his legate in Languedoc with a more muscular team of three. Significantly all of them were Cistercians, trusty servants of orthodoxy. They were: the Abbot of Citeaux, Arnold Amaury; a monk by the name of Brother Ralph; and a figure who was to prove the central *provocateur* in the events to come, Pierre de Castelnau, who besides being a monk from the great abbey of Fontfroide was also a trained lawyer—a fact that soon showed itself.

At first the three legates, led by Pierre de Castelnau, set about trying to win Count Raymond's cooperation by persuasion. Negotiations became protracted, and doubtless tedious, and before long achieved no more than token concessions from the count as he constantly played for time in order to avoid any binding commitments. As a result the years passed, and relationships between the count and Pierre de Castelnau grew progressively strained, with the lawyer-monk growing ever more exasperated by Raymond's prevarications. Finally, after four years, Raymond was cornered; the papal legates insisted that the count swear an oath of allegiance to the pope. At this point Raymond at last felt obliged to be resolute, and refused, whereupon Pierre promptly excommunicated him. His final words to the count are reported to have been: "He who strikes you dead will earn a blessing."

Raymond's response was to round up a token number of Cathars, sufficient to cause his excommunication to be lifted; after which he reverted to doing nothing, whereupon he was excommunicated a second time. Exasperation on both sides was by now reaching boiling-point, and when further discussions were resumed in the count's castle in St.-Gilles early in 1208 exchanges between the two men grew so heated that at one point Raymond is said to have threatened physical violence against the legate.

Then, on Sunday 13 January, negotiations broke down entirely. At dawn the following morning Pierre de Castelnau left on horseback for Rome and urgent discussions with the pope. Any traveller heading towards Arles, and eventually the port of Marseille, first needed to cross one of the branches of the Rhône (today the Petit Rhône) which flowed just a short distance to the east of St.-Gilles across the Camargue marshes. There was a ferry at this point, and a member of the legate's party would have ridden ahead to ensure that the craft was prepared and waiting for the papal entourage along with their horses and baggage. We have no precise details of the legate's arrival at the river bank, or whether he was compelled to wait a while before the ferry could take the party on board. All we know is that as Pierre de Castelnau was preparing to embark on that bleak midwinter dawn a hooded horseman rode up and drove a sword through him.

History is rich in coincidences. In England thirty-eight years earlier the Archbishop of Canterbury, Thomas à Becket, had been murdered with a sword in Canterbury Cathedral by knights who were apparently acting on the exasperated outburst of the English king Henry II: "who will rid me of this turbulent priest?" Pierre de Castelnau's murderer may never have heard of Becket, or of his fate, yet the parallel between the two events has many resonances. Neither King Henry nor Count Raymond is likely to have intended their outbursts to be acted upon literally. Both murders demonstrate how in royal and noble retinues there were courtiers and attendants whose loyalties were coupled with ruthless opportunism and self-interest. Both murders also had profound consequences for those widely blamed for ordering them: King Henry made public penance in Canterbury Cathedral; Count Raymond allowed himself to be stripped naked and thrashed in the abbey church of St.-Gilles in front of a papal legate and twenty bishops, and then swore allegiance to the pope, which he had previously refused to do. He was also compelled to forfeit seven of his castles as well as most of his estates, which were swallowed into the kingdom of France.

The longer-term outcome of Pierre de Castelnau's murder was more widespread, for it precipitated one of the most barbarous massacres in European history. Though compelled eventually to be whipped publicly as a display of contrition, Raymond had not immediately apologized, denying any responsibility for the murder—which may indeed have been the case. None the less, during the period of the count's prevarication Pope Innocent III decided to call for a crusade against the Cathars. They were to be destroyed. Nor was this to be an ordinary military campaign; in the eyes of the church a crusade, being a holy undertaking and therefore divinely blessed, allowed those taking part a number of extremely advantageous privileges. A soldier could be awarded forgiveness of all his sins, cancellation of personal debts, and—most tempting of all to any impoverished mercenary—the dazzling promise of booty from lands and property owned by the "enemy", in this case the disgraced Cathars. To become a crusader without being required to venture to far and alien lands: here was an invitation not to be missed.

Not surprisingly those who answered the call to arms were mainly adventurers, among them minor barons from northern France keen to grab as much of Languedoc as they could. To make matters worse they were led by a sadistic bigot; the man appointed to command the crusader army was the papal legate and former colleague of the murdered Pierre de Castelnau, Arnaud Amaury, the Cistercian Abbot of Citeaux. The crusaders' first target, in July 1209, was the city of Béziers. The place was scarcely a hotbed of heresy, containing what is believed to have been no more than five hundred Cathars. But when the demand for these to be handed over was refused, the order was given by Amaury to sack the city and slaughter the entire population, the abbot having declared, so it was reported, "Kill them all, for the Lord knows which are His." Contemporary sources give varying estimates of the numbers massacred, the most conservative being seven thousand, others calculating the number to be nearer forty thousand. It was a hideous day's work.

The horrific events at Béziers and the subsequent crushing of the Cathars throughout the region are matters that fall well outside the

borders of the Camargue. None the less the prosperity of St.-Gilles continued to be inextricably tied to the fortunes—or more often the ill-
fortunes—of successive counts of Toulouse, the town's feudal lords. For
them, as for the Cathars whom they were accused of supporting, the
noose tightened. In 1215, just seven years after the murder of the papal
legate, the pope convened the Fourth Lateran Council in which the orthodox dogma of the Catholic Church was spelt out, no longer per-
mitting variants of any kind. The outcome of this historic gathering
was the birth, twelve years later, of that most ugly instrument of religious repression, the Inquisition. From now on the Cathars were political and moral outlaws. Count Raymond's son and successor, Raymond
VII, who had struggled with some success to regain many of the lands
taken from his father, continued to stand out against the Albigensian
Crusade which he saw, accurately enough, as being led by adventurers
from the north using the issue of heresy as a mere pretext for grabbing
what lands they could. The count met his nemesis in 1226 when he
refused passage to the crusader army led by the French king Louis VIII,
defiantly closing the gates of the city of Avignon, which then lay within
his territories. A three-month siege followed, until finally the inhabitants were starved into submission. The king sacked the city, and in a
brutal repetition of the treatment that had been meted out to his father
in St.-Gilles, Count Raymond was compelled to be stripped to the waist
and whipped before the high altar of Avignon's cathedral with a rope
round his neck.

Raymond was also deprived of all the lands he had assiduously
clawed back in the years following his father's humiliation, being compelled to relinquish Languedoc to the French crown. The punishment
was even more severe: he was also made to relinquish the county of
Provence along with the city of Avignon—by now mostly reduced to
rubble, a condition from it never fully recovered until becoming the
home of the self-exiled papacy three quarters of a century later. (Then
of course, thanks to the popes, Avignon was to undergo a spectacular
change in fortunes, becoming one of the most glittering cities in
Europe—but that is quite another story.)

Though St.-Gilles never suffered from the crusade against the Cathars as severely as Avignon, the stigma of being the home town of the disgraced counts of Toulouse continued to hang over it. Fortunately its role as a centre of pilgrimage remained untouched by these brutal events. The abbey even gained an unexpected patron in the form of a citizen of the town. He was Gui Faucoi le Gros, or Foulque the Fat, a successful lawyer (hence perhaps the unflattering appellation) who rose to become secretary to the French king Louis IX (St. Louis), then papal legate in England, and finally was elected pope, as Clement IV. Foulque celebrated his success by showering gifts on the town of his birth, and his memory is preserved by a thirteenth-century three-storey mansion close to the abbey church known now as the Maison Romane and where tradition has it that he was born. Today the mansion is a museum which houses, along with the usual collection of stones and stuffed birds, displays of tools and rural artefacts illustrating traditional peasant occupations in the Camargue: agriculture, sheep-rearing, olive growing, vine-tending, fishing, as well as aspects of domestic life in the bleak marshlands long before visitors had found anything romantic about this marshy wilderness.

The abbey church of St.-Gilles is today a beautiful shell. A sad and sordid history has treated it as unjustly as those French barons from the north treated the Cathars. The French religious wars in the sixteenth century led to a Protestant army occupying the town, the soldiers then perpetrating a massacre almost as bloody as that which the crusader army had inflicted on the city of Béziers three centuries earlier. The tomb of St. Gilles disappeared. The priests and choir-boys of the abbey church were slaughtered, and their bodies thrown into a well, which is still visible in the crypt, though without bodies. Much of the crypt itself also survives, along with the staircase and ramp which the monks of the abbey once used as a means of entering the main church above. This, though, no longer exists. The Protestant army, in its reforming zeal, preferred to use it as a fortress rather than as a church, and demolished nearly all of it—mercifully, and perhaps more by oversight than intention, leaving only the great west front more or less intact.

Thus they limited their iconoclasm to hacking off a number of stone heads of Old Testament prophets, but otherwise managed to preserve one of the most magnificent ensembles of church sculpture of the Middle Ages in all Europe.

No gateway to the Camargue could be nobler than this.

Chapter Five

WHITE GOLD AND WHITE MONKS

The Camargue has no mountains—not surprisingly—so its inhabitants have created artificial ones instead. They are miniature mountains, it is true; and they are made of salt. They rise like a row of ghosts along the base of the triangle which is the delta of the Rhône, one group of them at the eastern extremity of the Camargue close to the mouth of Le Grand Rhône, the other bordering on a patchwork of creeks and canals far to the west. Locally these salt mountains are called *camelles* because against the background of sea and sky they can be seen as a Bedouin camel-train processing across a shimmering desert. Or so they say. But fanciful images aside, these *camelles* are certainly among the strangest features of the Camargue landscape, not least because they are so un-expected amid the wilderness of swamp and water. There is an eerie beauty about them—so much pristine whiteness which in the shadows can suddenly give way to the softest shades of blue, yellow and green.

These salt mountains are the product of the sea. In the spring of each year sea-water is let into a grid of shallow pans, called *salins*, to a precisely-controlled depth. Over the following months the water steadily evaporates under the summer sun. And in the process a curiously beautiful transformation takes place; the sea-water in the *salins* turns delicately rose-coloured. At first sight this phenomenon can seem to be a trick of the light since nothing is visible which might have brought about such a transformation. In fact the agent that has caused this change is indeed invisible except under a microscope: it is a variety of algae called *dunaliella salina*, which eventually disappears as the salt condenses and finally crystallizes. Then in September the salt is raked from the *salins* and piled into these long chains of salt mountains to dry out until ready to be marketed either for industrial or domestic purposes.

Sea-salt is the oldest commercial industry of the Camargue, and traditionally the chief source of its wealth, earning itself the name "white gold" as early as the Middle Ages. It has also long been a key element in the survival of Camargue wild-life. Being shallow the salt-pans are a haven for wading birds hunting for tiny molluscs or shrimps—avocets, egrets, stilts, sandpipers and in particular scarlet flamingos—the precise control of water levels being as vital for the well-being of flamingos as it is for the production of salt.

The two areas covered by the *salins*, in the eastern and western extremities of the Camargue, are enormous. Each is estimated to be large enough to hold the entire city of Paris—a strange calculation to have been made, yet apparently true. That said, visiting either of these areas is less likely to conjure up images of Paris than of a lunar landscape. Lost amid a grid system in the middle of nowhere, you can feel this to be one of the loneliest places on earth.

Two small towns stand guard over the *salins*. In the west, rising out of the marshes, is the extraordinary walled town of Aigues-Mortes, the port built by the most saintly king France ever had, Louis IX, and from where he launched two crusades to the Holy Land (see the following chapter). Then, at the eastern end of the Camargue the salt-pans bear the name of the town which presides over them, Salin-de-Giraud. It would be a test of ingenuity to imagine a place less like Aigues-Mortes in appearance. Whereas the latter is a medieval bastion sprouting turrets and battlements, Salin-de-Giraud is a sprawling industrial village. It was built largely in the nineteenth century, formally laid-out in a grid pattern exactly like the salt-pans themselves, so that it resembles a well-planned but rather soulless suburb which somehow ought not to be in the Camargue at all. In fact it has always existed for one reason only: it has provided housing for those workers and their families who came here to service the largest salt-works in Europe, as Salin-de-Giraud was—at least until very recently.

Soulless the place may seem at first, yet it has one particular claim to be special. Most of the inhabitants of Salin-de-Giraud today are the descendants of immigrant workers who in the course of the last hundred years or so came here to seek employment in the flourishing salt industry, and then settled. They are for the most part Spanish, Italian, Armenian and, in particular Greek. And of the many hundreds of Greeks living and working here the largest homogeneous group originates from one small island in the Dodecanese lying close to the Turkish coast. The island is Calymnos, which is squeezed between the larger islands of Leros and Cos, a little to the north of Rhodes. Salin-de-Giraud is Little Calymnos, with its own Greek island traditions, its festivities, food, music and dances. Salin-de-Giraud's inhabitants have even built their own small Greek Orthodox church, though its blue roof and white walls are the only echoes it has to offer of those little Byzantine chapels which contribute so much to the character of the Greek islands. Furthermore, if the Calymnos community here is occupied in a single industry, salt, then the habit of being engaged in a monoculture is one that they brought with them from the eastern Aegean, where the traditional occupation of the menfolk of Calymnos has long been sponge-fishing. One product of the sea became exchanged for another.

The Camargue salt industry can be traced back many centuries before Greek and other foreign workers migrated here. A short distance south of the fortified town of Aigues-Mortes is a canal which runs southwards between high banks separating it from an expanse of salt-pans and shallow lagoons that stretch almost to the sea. After five or six miles the canal turns sharply eastwards at an isolated spot close to what was once a small settlement on the edge of the marshes. It then heads north-east towards one of the two branches of the Rhône, the Petit Rhône, passing on the way the remains of an ancient fort. Seen from the ground there seems nothing particularly remarkable about this area of the Camargue; it is merely another stretch of reed-beds and lagoons over which herons and marsh harriers patrol in search of small prey. But a look at a detailed map reveals something else: a clue to a significant moment in the history of this region. All three places—the canal, the small settlement and the ancient fort—bear the same name: Peccais.

Place-names linger on long after their original meaning is lost. The name Peccais is in fact a surviving witness to the earliest record we have of a salt industry in the Camargue. We know that a man by the name of Peccaius was a Roman engineer at the beginning of the Christian era, in the fourth century, and that he was placed in charge of salt production in the Camargue. The appointment would have come from Arles, then the Roman capital of the entire western empire, and very possibly from the Emperor Constantine himself.

In other words the Camargue, which had long been the granary of the Roman armies in Gaul, was about to supply another of the most valuable commodities for the Roman kitchen. Here in this remote region of marshland which still bears his name, Peccaius the engineer laid out his salt-pans and so began the production of sea-salt which continues to this day.

Little more than a century and a half later barbarian hordes swarmed across southern Gaul, and the Roman Empire fell into a state of terminal collapse. It was the beginning of what we have come to describe as the Dark Ages. And not surprisingly there is a black hole in our knowledge of the salt industry, and indeed of the Camargue in general, persisting for several hundred years. Saracen invasions from Spain and North Africa caused further strife and disorder. Arles itself was attacked and overrun many times. Yet during the course of these dark centuries a new force of order began to make its mark on the region. That new force was the monasteries, and in particular those belonging to the Benedictine Order inspired by the example of St. Benedict at the abbey of Monte Cassino in southern Italy, which he had founded in the sixth century. In the Dark Ages monasteries became islands of stability in a sea of anarchy, as well as cells of faith and of learning. They kept Christianity alive at a time when it might have withered away. Wielding massive spiritual authority they were able to establish a code of morality and behaviour which became one of the most vital keys to the shaping of a new and more civilized Europe.

Equally important to that new Europe was that, by their own labours and the promotion of skills of all kinds—building and agriculture among them—Benedictine monasteries came to play a crucial role in revitalizing the economic life of the Christian world. They took over the economic life of this region, as well as much of the rest of Europe. And in the Camargue that meant, most of all, salt.

From as early as the eighth century we find records of generous donations being made by local rulers to recently-founded abbeys. In economic as well as spiritual terms the monasteries were beginning to be seen as a good investment. In the year 822 the Emperor Charlemagne's son and heir, Louis I ("the Pious") made a handsome gift to an abbey at Narbonne, down the coast from the Camargue, the nature of the gift being highly significant. It was a grant of salt-pans. Other donations by rulers followed regularly, made to a variety of abbeys in the area, until by the middle of the eleventh century we have a record of a gift to a local abbey made by the most powerful feudal lord in the region, the count of Toulouse. The record details how the count donated a salt-pan and also describes how the salt was actually produced. It was the triple method of concentration, condensation and crystallization: precisely the method still employed in the *salins* of the Camargue today.

So, we know that by the early Middle Ages the production of "white gold" was already a sophisticated and highly profitable industry. And if further proof were needed we need only to look at the rise of the Venetian Republic during this same period. Its wealth was founded on salt. The production of salt from the Venetian lagoon was so profitable that it subsidized most of the republic's ship-building activities, enabling the Venetian fleet to establish a Mediterranean empire which held "the gorgeous east in fee/And was the safeguard of the west," as Wordsworth was to describe it.

In an age of refrigerators, deep-freezers and canned foodstuffs it is easy to overlook the fact that salt, the great preservative, was for centuries among the most valued commodities of life; and to have access to it was to obtain incalculable wealth and influence. The early monasteries, as much by opportunism and organizational skills as by hard labour, took full advantage of this need. And by a wondrous slice of irony their commercial success was to a large extent made possible by the requirement that abbeys be established in isolated places far removed from urban life and the evils of this world. Salt, after all, was not a commodity to be found in big cities.

There was one early abbey in the Camargue which grew immensely rich and powerful largely through its control of salt production in much of the Rhône delta. This was the abbey of Psalmodi. Fluctuations in the course of the great river, as well as the continual shifting of the coast-line, have dealt brutally with so many ancient buildings in these unforgiving marshlands, as we know from the disappearance of the Roman villas which once graced the area. Yet this particular abbey has not entirely vanished. The same detailed map that identifies the Roman salt-pans of Peccais also identifies an isolated farmhouse a few miles to the north of Aigues-Mortes. In small letters one can make out the name "Mas Psalmody". The spelling may have altered slightly, but there can be no mistaking the site. The place is privately owned now, and its entrance heavily gated and protected by a loud security alarm. Fortunately there are other ways of accessing what the inquisitive visitor is denied, such as a low-flying helicopter. Looking down from so privileged a vantage-point the lay-out of the ancient site becomes even clearer than it would be on the ground. The abbey must originally have been spread over a large area, though little more than foundations have survived.

These include what was evidently a church, centrally placed among numerous other buildings.

Today the place is several miles inland and surrounded by canals and swampy fields. But from the air one can sees quite clearly from the shape and lay-out of the site that the abbey and its immediately surrounding land was once an island. In fact, one of the early donations to the abbey, in the year 788, describes it as *Insula Psalmodia*. The island would have been encircled by salt-marsh and broad lagoons, with the coastline somewhat closer than it is now. One of the lesser branches of the Rhône ran conveniently close by, essential for the transport of salt and other produce and goods inland to Arles or to Beaucaire.

Psalmodi was a Benedictine abbey founded as early as the eighth century. It rose rapidly to such a position of power that at the beginning of the ninth century the Emperor Charlemagne could speak of its fame, while the abbot of that time, a certain Theodorimus, boasted that his monastery supported 140 monks and was one of the largest in Europe. Its prosperity continued and expanded for many centuries to come until by the end of the eleventh century Psalmodi had control of no fewer than sixty churches and priories. Eventually by the thirteenth century that number had swollen to ninety properties, and these now stretched from the Alps to the Pyrenees.

Such was the power of salt.

Yet the great era of the Camargue "salt abbeys" came many centuries after the founding of Psalmodi, and it was brought about through the arrival of the Cistercians, the "white monks". The Cistercian Order, founded by Bernard, abbot of Clairvaux, early in the twelfth century, was an austere breakaway from the Benedictines who were regarded as having lost sight of their spiritual calling by indulging in a "soft" life devoted to plainsong and books, and in an appetite for rich food and luxury goods. The most pertinent issue dividing the two orders was the value or otherwise of manual labour in monastic life. Stipulated in the Rule of St. Benedict as an important ingredient in a monk's spiritual day, by the twelfth century manual labour had come to play little or no part in the daily routine of a Benedictine monk. Physical work in the

fields was increasingly being allocated either to lay brothers or to labourers with no connection to a monastery whatsoever beyond that of being
serfs tied by feudal laws to working an abbey's fields or tending its livestock. It may well be that the monks of Psalmodi "went soft" in precisely
this way, so contributing to what we know to have been a collapse of
their fortunes in the century following.

The Cistercians, by contrast, interpreted the Rule of St. Benedict
to the very letter. For them work in the fields was an essential part of
every monk's day. Manual labour was a form of prayer. Life devoted to
God was supposed to be hard, and in their rigorous asceticism they
modelled themselves on St. Jerome and the desert fathers. The more
remote and inhospitable the landscape the more appropriate it was as
a place in which to live and work, and to worship God. Physical work
was a test of a monk's spirit and of his manual skills. The result was that
the Cistercians soon became excellent farmers, invariably in regions
where no men in their right minds had ever considered trying to farm
at all. At the same time they were practical enough to ensure that whatever wilderness they chose to inhabit possessed certain basic requirements: this generally meant pasture for their sheep and an ample supply
of running water, preferably a river.

The Camargue fulfilled all these requirements perfectly. Fresh water
was available everywhere, from the various branches of the Rhône and
innumerable creeks and canals. A little inland from the sea there were
also moist pastures ideal for grazing sheep. And there was the added
bonus of plentiful salt-water lagoons which could be made to produce
quantities of "white gold".

The first Cistercians are believed to have settled in the Camargue
around the year 1143, in the lifetime of their founder. The site where
they built their first abbey was well-chosen. It was situated on the northern bank of a branch of the Rhône (now a navigable canal linking
Aigues-Mortes with St.-Gilles) at a place they called Franquevaux, today
a small agricultural community close to the canal. To the south of the
river lay the salt-marshes and lagoons which the monks soon learnt to
utilize and transform into *salins*. But on the north side of the river lay

quite a different terrain. This was pasture land, suitably remote from human habitation, yet on slightly higher ground not flooded by sea-water and hence ideal for grazing animals—cattle and in particular sheep. The Cistercians were already proving to be expert sheep-farmers, especially in England where several "wool abbeys" had already been founded, among them Rievaulx in Yorkshire in 1131. At Franquevaux the combination of salt from one side of the river and livestock on the other supplied the perfect answer to the Cistercians' requirement to be self-sufficient: beef and mutton from the grazing-lands could be preserved during the winter months by salt that was readily on hand, and which also enabled the monks to flavour a variety of cheeses from the milk those animals supplied. Besides, wool from the same sheep could be woven and tailored to make the white robes on which the order insisted, making a proud virtue of the wool being undyed and therefore "natural" (unlike the Benedictines who preferred their robes to be "unnatural", being of wool that had been pre-dyed black).

Unlike Psalmodi, little survives of Franquevaux abbey; the unforgiving Camargue terrain has done its work again. A fragment of the monks' church remains in one of the village houses—disguised for much of its recent existence as a wine-cellar. Not that this new role is quite as sacrilegious as it may sound, as the monks are known to have planted vines on their low-lying estates. In fact wine made from their grapes is likely to have been the precursors of the local *vin de sable*, as it is called, a somewhat thin beverage which is still produced here, much of it under the auspices of the salt companies of the Camargue.

Fourteen years after the Cistercians founded their abbey at Franquevaux a larger party of monks, as many as one hundred and fifty of them, arrived from the monastery of Bonnevaux, in the mountains to the north, in order to establish another religious house in the Camargue marshlands. Whether their motive was the challenge of yet another inhospitable wilderness, or perhaps a more commercial consideration of exploiting the local salt-marshes in the wake of their brethren's success at Franquevaux, we can only guess. One event had taken place in the interim which may have acted as a spur to the newcomers: this was the death of their founding father and inspiration, Bernard of Clairvaux, four years earlier in 1153. The site they chose was on the banks of yet another branch of the Rhône, though unlike Franquevaux it lay deep in the heart of the salt-marshes south-east of the vast central lagoon of the Camargue known today as the Etang de Vaccarès. The site was called Ulmet, and within a very short time it appears to have grown into the most important of the Cistercian salt abbeys.

But the success of Ulmet was short-lived. Within forty years the treacherous river which the monks had chosen to be their lifeline burst its banks and flooded the newly-built abbey, destroying everything except the monks themselves, who fled to set up their religious house elsewhere in the delta. Today Ulmet is another entry in small print on the local map. A mere hillock commemorates the former monastery, situated on land which is within the present-day Réserve Nationale de Camargue whose headquarters and information centre lie a short distance to the north at La Capelière.

The branch of the Rhône which destroyed Ulmet concluded its fickle journey through the centuries by finally drying up three hundred years later. The lower reaches of the river to the south of Ulmet survived as a canal, as it still does, snaking its way towards the sea past one of the Camargue's many ruined medieval towers, and continuing to bear the name on the map: Vieux Rhône.

This whole area to the south and east of the Etang de Vaccarès remains one of the most appealing in the whole of the Camargue. Unlike so much of the region it is also accessible. A minor road, the D36B, runs south from the village of Villeneuve, leading eventually to the town of Salin-de-Giraud and beyond it the lunar landscape of salt-pans, and finally to the nature reserve of La Palissade occupying the last tip of marshland before the sea next to where the Grand Rhône ends its five-hundred-mile journey from the Swiss Alps. In the course of twenty miles the road passes through terrain of startling variety, which confounds any view that Camargue is simply an extended soggy marsh. By offering constant surprises it is a journey which manages to encapsulate the charm and magic of the whole delta. It begins in an area of dense woodland which might be anywhere in northern Europe, before giving way to patches of marsh, scrub and secret lagoons which are speckled with wildlife. Then suddenly the tamarisk thickets part and the road breaks into the open skirting the very edge of the great lagoon, the Vaccarès. Here grey herons and white egrets stalk the shallows, and flocks of wild duck in their thousands dot the surface—sometimes calm and silvery as a sheet of glass, at other times ruffled into scores of tiny waves by the mistral, which regularly hurtles across the Camargue.

Further south, past La Capelière and beyond the site of Ulmet abbey, a signpost reads "La Digue à la Mer". This is the sea dyke built in the mid-nineteenth century to control salt-water flooding. Following the sign an even narrower road threads its way through scrub and marshland before emerging as if launched on to an apron stage; and suddenly we are gazing out over a pattern of lagoons spreading out in every direction. The horizon is broken only by distant lighthouses along the sea dyke, and even further away to the west by the silhouette of the fortified church of Les Saintes-Maries. At this point the road abruptly ends, breaking into several broad gravel tracks which fan out in different directions across a web of raised dykes that divide up the lagoons.

Only a short distance from these serene lagoons the Cistercian monks of Ulmet were driven from their abbey by the violence of water bursting from the swollen river. Yet, in spite of having been flooded out by one branch of the Rhône, the monks were intrepid enough to establish themselves beside another branch of the same river. The new site was on the west bank of the Petit Rhône some ten miles upstream from Les Saintes-Maries-de-la-Mer, on a sharp bend of the river. The name of the place, Sylvéréal, gives the clue to its origin as well as to its habitat. The area must at this time have been forested, and been a royal possession. In fact an abbey, or at least a priory, is known to have been founded here in the twelfth century by King Alfonso of Aragon whose Spanish kingdom at this time was expanding rapidly north of the Pyrenees and eastwards along the Mediterranean coast to include much of what is now Languedoc. We do not know the precise date of its foundation, but the likelihood is that it was not long before the arrival of the large number of monks from a flooded Ulmet. They would have chosen a religious house that was recently established and well-enough endowed to support and accommodate them.

So Sylvéréal became the third of the Cistercian "salt abbeys" to be established in the Camargue.

Sadly, like the other two, Sylvéréal has all but vanished, apart from the remains of yet another defensive tower close to the river. The local map points to what used to be here in the form of two ghostly entries close by: they are farmhouses called respectively La Grande Abbaye and (a little further downriver) La Petite Abbaye. Once again names have survived when places have not. First the Greeks and the Romans, then the Benedictines, and now the Cistercians: all have gone with the wind. The Camargue today is presided over by so many disembodied spirits of the past, their presence testified only by their names on road-signs pointing to next-to-nothing.

There is yet one more ethereal spirit that haunts the salt-pans. The Museum of the Camargue, situated in its long converted sheepfold at the Mas du Pont de Rousty to the south-west of Arles, displays a *borne*—a boundary stone—bearing a distinctive carved motif, an eight-pointed star which was the emblem of the Knights of St. John of Jerusalem, generally known as the Knights Hospitallers (though they had also been the Knights of Rhodes and the Knights of Malta). A boundary marker can only mean that they owned land: in fact the Hospitallers came to own large tracts of land in the Camargue, operating from fortified settlements known as *commanderies* and making their own contribution to agriculture and almost certainly to the salt industry. Like the Knights Templar they were a military order governed by monastic rules, and they were a product of the crusades and of the establishment of a Christian kingdom in Palestine. In the early years following the First Crusade and the conquest of Jerusalem in 1099 the Hospitallers performed the key role of protecting and caring for the growing number of Christian pilgrims who were beginning to flock to Jerusalem and to the lands of the Bible.

How they came to find themselves here in the Camargue is one of those anomalies of history which abound in the Middle Ages. And here we need to backtrack a little. Inevitably it was by and large the wealthy who could afford a pilgrimage to the Holy Land; hence a combination of riches and piety soon led to handsome donations being made to the Hospitallers out of gratitude and genuine respect, until by the mid-twelfth century the order had come to possess considerable wealth as well as large tracts of lands right across Europe. These properties swelled even more after their fellow military order, the Knights Templar, was forcibly dissolved in 1312 as a result of one of the most cynically dishonest trials in history instigated by an impoverished French king who wanted their money—as a result of which many of the Templars' lands and possessions were handed over to the grateful Hospitallers.

Precisely where those lands were, what the knights grew on them, and where precisely their *commanderies* were, remains another batch of puzzles. All we know is that they were here. The carved *borne* displayed in the Museum of the Camargue remains a lone and tantalizing clue to a mystery that is unlikely ever to be solved.

Romans, Benedictines, Cistercians, Hospitallers: all of them profited greatly from the "white gold" of the Camargue. And they were richly rewarded for their services—the last three of them at least. As producers of so valuable a commodity the salt abbeys were awarded extensive privileges by way of inducements, as well as grants from the kings of France. The abbeys paid no tithes or taxes on the goods they produced (which included wheat and wine as well as salt), in addition to which they were free to transport their produce to the markets of the region without the customary payment of tolls.

The Cistercians were particularly singled out in terms of privileges. The special favours showered on them were to a large extent a reward for the continued support the order gave to the papacy and the French crown in mounting the Albigensian Crusade against the heretical

Cathars. The Cistercians' founder, Bernard of Clairvaux, who loathed any deviation from strict religious orthodoxy with a furious passion, had preached vigorously against the Cathars in a visit to their heartland of Languedoc. Then, at the very gateway of the Camargue, at St.-Gilles, the assassination of the papal legate transformed the whole campaign against the Cathars from preaching to military action. In the course of that campaign it had been the Cistercian abbot of Cîteaux, Arnaud Amaury, who led a murderous army from northern France to suppress Catharism by force, leading to the indiscriminate slaughter of the entire population of Béziers (described in the previous chapter). Finally, it had been another former Cistercian monk, Jacques Fournier, who in his capacity as Chief Inquisitor effectively signed the death warrant on the last of the Cathars early in the fourteenth century. Fournier was created a cardinal for his services by the Avignon pope of the day, John XXII, and shortly afterwards became elected as his successor, taking the name Benedict XII.

Admirable farmers and inspired architects though they were, religious tolerance was not a virtue inscribed in any creed of the Cistercians. Only unswerving orthodoxy was permitted.

The rewards cascading on to the salt abbeys of the Camargue between the twelfth and fourteenth centuries were a small price for the French crown to pay in comparison to the colossal benefits which the monarchy gained from that loyal Cistercian support in the Albigensian Crusade. It was the suppression of the Cathars and the consequent seizing of southern lands by opportunist northern lords which effectively stifled the political ambitions of the south for ever, as Languedoc became annexed by France.

The Cistercian abbeys, both those in the Camargue and elsewhere throughout Europe, grew inordinately wealthy. Theirs was indeed a story of rags to riches, in the end not unlike the fortunes of the Benedictine Order from which the Cistercians chose so haughtily to distance themselves. For a religious order founded on the principles of poverty, isolation and self-sufficiency, here was a puzzling contradiction, one which its founder, St. Bernard of Clairvaux, would have

Guardian of the salt road, the Tour Carbonnière.

needed all his celebrated eloquence to resolve.

Not surprisingly the success of the Camargue salt industry attracted covetous eyes: it was inevitable that such a lucrative trade would not be allowed to remain untaxed for ever. It was just a question of time before some local ruler would be dramatically in need of cash. The moment came around the year 1250 when the count of Provence, Charles of Anjou, who was also the brother of the king of France, urgently required funds to mount a military campaign in southern Italy, the purpose of which was to secure the kingdom of Naples, of which—improbable though it may sound—he was the titular ruler, in addition to being the lord of Provence. Charles' method of fundraising was to levy a tax, which came to be known as the *gabelle*, and it was levied on all salt from the eastern region of the Camargue, which conveniently lay within his Provençal domain.

Politically it was a master-stroke. The campaign in Italy succeeded, and the idea of a "salt tax" took hold. It was easy money; and no ruling dynasty in Europe craved money more hungrily than the kings of France. At this time the French crown owned only a fragment of the Camargue, a stretch of marshland sold by the abbot of Psalmodi to King Louis IX so that he might build a port from which to launch a new crusade (described in the following chapter). Louis himself was more concerned with the Holy Land than with salt, and the nearby salt-pans of Peccais, which dated from Roman times, continued to be the property of the Benedictine abbey of Psalmodi in conjunction with two local lords.

This state of affairs was not to last. Half a century later a famously impecunious French monarch, Louis' grandson Philip IV (the same monarch who was responsible for crushing the Knights Templar), succeeded in acquiring the Peccais salt-pans. He proceeded to increase hugely the area covered by them, and hence the quantity of salt produced annually, securing one-seventh of the production for himself to dispose of as he chose. At the same time Philip made a treaty with his relative, the count of Anjou, for joint control of the entire Camargue salt market, ensuring that the extended Peccais *salins* (which he now owned) would from now onwards supply no less than two-thirds of the salt required for the whole of France. Within half a century the institution of the *gabelle*, which the count of Provence had put in place a hundred years earlier, became officially a privilege of the French crown. And so it remained until the French Revolution more than four centuries later.

One surviving monument in the western Camargue demonstrates the importance of the salt industry in those opportunist times, as well as the hazards attendant on so lucrative a trade. In the midst of the marshlands a few miles north of Aigues-Mortes, on what is now a minor road, the eye is suddenly arrested by the sight of a gaunt squat tower standing defiantly in the roadway. This is the Tour Carbonnière, and it was built at about the time the French king acquired the right to supply two-thirds of the nation's requirement of salt from the Peccais *salins*, which were now royal property.

This great tower would have held a permanent garrison of soldiers, their primary function being to guard what became known as the "salt road". Originally this road linked the salt-pans of Peccais to the monastery of Psalmodi just two miles further north—this at a time when the abbey owned the *salins* before they became the property of the French crown. But by the fourteenth century the salt road bypassed Psalmodi and led straight to the city of Nîmes, which was the entrepôt from where this most highly-prized commodity of the Middle Ages was distributed to the markets and kitchens of an entire nation.

Today the Tour Carbonnière is a lonely anachronism. But in its day it performed a vital role: it safeguarded the culinary needs of two-thirds of France as well as ensuring a healthy purse for its monarch. It was the Camargue's fortress of "white gold".

Chapter Six

AIGUES-MORTES AND THE
CRUSADES

Heading westwards across the Camargue from the bridge over the Petit Rhône at Sylvéréal, the road threads its way past small lagoons and marshy fields and then skirts an unexpected forest of pines. They are umbrella pines, which are among the most lordly of Mediterranean trees whether in the centre of Rome, along the coast of North Africa or on a remote Greek island: but here in the Camargue they can offer a bonus as the eye catches sight of a dense colony of egrets perched high among the canopy of branches, adding a dazzle of white to the foliage as if a heavy snowfall had descended on a single tree. It is one of those dramatic surprises which make up the magic of the Camargue.

A short distance beyond the forest lies the turning to the north along the old salt road towards the Tour Carbonnière and Psalmodi, and eventually to Nîmes. But in the opposite direction, to the left, the road leads after a mile or so to the most dramatic spectacle in the whole of the Camargue. This is the fortified town of Aigues-Mortes, which stands like an operatic stage-set in the midst of an expanse of lagoon and marshland, giving the impression that time became frozen at the moment when those massive ramparts were constructed more than seven hundred years ago. Here, as visitors, we are invited to step into the Middle Ages.

Aigues-Mortes is the Camargue's dark sentinel. It was constructed for one specific reason alone. In the thirteenth century the French king, Louis IX (later canonized as St. Louis) urgently needed a port on the Mediterranean from which to launch a fresh crusade to the Holy Land. All suitable sea-ports in the region, including Marseille, lay outside the French royal domain. The most likely area available to him was the Camargue. Much of the Rhône delta had recently fallen by good fortune into the king's hands as a result of the treaty which in 1229 brought an end to the Albigensian Crusade against the heretical Cathars, as a result of which lands previously held by the disgraced counts of Toulouse, supposed supporters of the Cathars, became absorbed into the kingdom of France (as described in Chapter 4).

On the other hand the Camargue itself, consisting for the most part of swamp and salt-marsh, was scarcely the ideal territory for constructing a port from which to launch a crusading armada. Only one place offered the prospect of being potentially suitable: this was a small fishing village known as the Port des Eaux-Mortes (or Aigues-Mortes in the local language) which lay on the edge of a lagoon described at the time as the Etang de l'Abbé. In other words, although the area was now part of the kingdom of France, it was also owned privately by the church in the shape of a nearby monastery. The religious house in question was none other than the great salt abbey of Psalmodi. As it transpired, this proved to be greatly to King Louis' advantage. Only a few decades earlier the abbey was known to have controlled as many as ninety properties extending from the Alps to the Pyrenees; none the less, for reasons which are far from clear, Psalmodi was by now in severe financial straits, with large debts to banks in the region and unpaid loans from the powerful Knights Templar. Not surprisingly the French king's advisers seized the opportunity to open negotiations between Louis and the abbot of Psalmodi, and as a result in 1240 it was agreed that the village of Aigues-Mortes, along with "the territories in which it is placed" (in other words the waterways giving access to the sea) would be surrendered by the abbot to the French crown—although the abbey wisely retained possession of the neighbouring salt-pans along with fishing rights.

The rebuilding of Aigues-Mortes as a fortress capable of housing and catering for the French king and his family, along with an entire crusading army, could now begin. It was a formidable task and it needed to be done rapidly, the predicament of the Crusader kingdom in Palestine being perilous in the extreme. (In fact, no more than eight years were to elapse between Louis' original purchase of the site as a mere fishing village and the ambitious launching of the crusading fleet.)

We know a great deal more about Louis IX than we do about any other European monarch of the time, largely because his close friend and counsellor, Jean de Joinville, wrote a celebrated biography of him. Louis was by any standards a man of the highest moral calibre, the more remarkable in an age when probity was less characteristic of European rulers than rapacity and opportunism. Voltaire in the eighteenth century offered a typically double-edged assessment of Louis as a man who "seemed to be a prince destined to reform Europe, had it been capable of being reformed." His piety took many forms, from ordering the construction of the Sainte-Chapelle in Paris as his private chapel, to the costly purchase from Constantinople of what he was assured was Christ's Crown of Thorns, along with a substantial fragment of the Holy Cross, both relics having been obtained originally from the Basilica of Mount Sion in Jerusalem—which gave them a certain credibility in contemporary eyes. Then a near-fatal illness in 1244 further strengthened Louis' resolve to lead his crusade to the Holy Land should he recover. And it was in the same year, having survived, that he made the binding commitment to do so by "taking the cross". These were beleaguered times for Christendom, and the crusading spirit needed ur-

gently to be rekindled. Jerusalem had already fallen to the armies of
Islam, and the Christians' hold on their remaining lands in Palestine
was looking ever more fragile. The general unease over the security of
Christian territory was further increased by the mounting danger of
massive Mongol invasions of Europe from the east.

For a zealous Christian king, who was also the most powerful and
prestigious ruler in Europe, a crusade to regain the Bible lands, to be led
by none other than Louis himself, seemed altogether the most glorious
and godly ambition a monarch could have, and one that he was determined to fulfil. And the new port of Aigues-Mortes was to be where the
great enterprise was to be launched.

Louis had come to the throne of France at the tender age of eleven,
and for a number of years the country was effectively ruled by his
mother, Blanche of Castile, who was the granddaughter of Eleanor of
Aquitaine and King Henry II of England. She was a forceful lady as
well as being deeply religious, and Louis' own unswerving piety was a
quality he doubtless acquired from his mother. As a politician she was
also shrewd enough to arrange a highly suitable marriage for the young
king. His bride was Marguerite of Provence, a daughter of the count of
Provence, a territory that lay on the borders of the recently-acquired
French lands in Languedoc. Hence it was a highly auspicious match: if
medieval royal marriages were sometimes negotiated in the manner of
a chess game, here was a brilliantly advantageous move by Queen
Blanche which brought the prospect of Provence becoming absorbed
into France an important step closer, particularly since the bride's father,
the count, had no surviving sons.

He did, on the other hand, have not just one daughter, but four.
All of them, what is more, were famously beautiful. In fact, so famous
was their beauty that all four became married to kings—an achievement which may never have been equalled in the entire history of the
royal marriage market. Marguerite was the eldest daughter, and on her
marriage to Louis in the year 1234 she automatically became queen of
France (proceeding to bear him eleven children, and still managing to
outlive him). The second daughter, Eleanor of Provence, was to marry

King Henry III of England. The third, Sanchia of Provence, became the wife of Richard, Duke of Cornwall, who had a serious claim (at least in his own eyes) to be king of the Germans; while the youngest daughter, Beatrice of Provence, became married to King Charles I of Sicily. The count of Provence had good reason to be proud of his offspring, even if a son and heir was not among them.

It was in 1240, six years after his marriage to Marguerite, that Louis sealed the purchase of Aigues-Mortes from the abbot of Psalmodi. It was a purchase, however, which came at a considerable price. This small fishing village in the Camargue marshes was far from being the ideal location from which to launch an impressive crusading fleet to the Holy Land. There was no inner harbour to speak of; only vessels of shallow draught could make it this far from the sea. As for the outer harbour, it was too far away to be of much use except to fishing-boats. Furthermore it opened directly on to the Mediterranean, and constantly silted up. The village of Aigues-Mortes itself was virtually an island surrounded by salt-water that was brackish and shallow, and accordingly there was always going to be a severe shortage of drinking water, certainly far from adequate for the requirements of any future crusading army.

Then there was the infamous north wind, the mistral, which regularly hurtled down the Rhône valley and across the bleak marshes, bending trees, creating sand-storms whipped up from the coastal dunes, and generally contributing to the multiple miseries of the place. Besides, there was disease; the Middle Ages may not have known that malaria was carried by mosquitoes, but those affected certainly knew about malaria, generally referred to as swamp fever. And people died just the same.

The village, as it still was, had been constructed on the edge of an *étang*, a shallow lake separated from the open sea by low-lying stretches of land that were themselves divided up by narrow threads of water known as *graux*. These slender channels, like the harbour itself, required constant dredging. It was a landscape of impermanence: the wind, the river and the sea conspired to make the whole environment unstable.

There were urgent priorities for Louis before the place could be made navigable, let alone habitable. A mole needed to be constructed to control the invasions of the sea. But this required stone, as did the road which had to be laid linking the mole to dry land—if, that is, any land in this flood-prone region could reasonably be described as "dry". What was more, there was no suitable local stone: hence it had to be obtained from the limestone quarries thirty miles inland near Beaucaire, then transported by barge down one of the lesser branches of the Rhône (today the Canal du Rhône) which at least ran conveniently close to the village. None the less it was a laborious and costly process. An even more urgent priority was to create an inner harbour close to the village in which large vessels could be moored. The stretch of water immediately to the south (today this has reverted to being two lagoons, the Etang de la Ville and the Etang de la Marette) proved to be deep enough provided it was constantly dredged, This inner harbour could then be linked by a channel running south-west directly to the sea towards what is now the port of Le Grau-du-Roi, though in the thirteenth century the coastline was appreciably closer to Aigues-Mortes than it is today.

We have no record of precisely how many years these large-scale engineering works may have taken: only that they were achieved, and that as a result maritime contact with the outside world was finally established. So, it cannot have been more than eight years, which is impressive given the scale of the operation.

Once materials could be transported by river from the north and by sea from the south, the transformation of Aigues-Mortes into a bastion and garrison town was able to progress in earnest. King Louis' first requirement was for a headquarters in this remote outpost of his kingdom, somewhere that would also be a fortress to protect the new port as well as provide accommodation for himself and his queen during the lengthy period before the crusading fleet could at last be assembled, made ready and finally launched. The result was the construction of a grim edifice which is still the dominant landmark in the town, a cylindrical slab of bare stone with walls twenty feet thick. It was known at first simply as the King's Tower, but later re-labelled the Constance

Tower—the Tour de Constance—named for no obvious reason after a daughter of Louis' royal ancestor, Louis VI, except that she had married the count of Toulouse. So at least there was a local connection, even though it was with a now-disgraced family.

Not surprisingly considering the bulk of the tower, by the time Louis was ready to launch his crusade in 1248 there was still no stone spare for building anything other than the Tour de Constance. The ramparts that were built at this time were still of wood, the timber having been cut from forests requisitioned from rebel landowners found guilty of supporting the heretical Cathars. Furthermore, the labourers who actually built the ramparts were themselves conscripts, also for the most part former Cathars. Thus, the price of heresy in Languedoc continued to be a heavy burden on the shoulders of the local inhabitants, although much to the advantage of the king of France.

It is easy to underestimate the magnitude of this building enterprise. In the course of no more than a few years Louis was undertaking to construct a "new town" in a malarial swamp with no building materials readily available except mud and reeds. The town was to be capable of housing the king himself, his family, servants and retainers, and ultimately an entire crusading army—all of whom had to be housed, watered and fed. The mammoth scale of the construction work was only part of the operation; what was also urgently required was a large quantity of people of different skills, from doctors to bakers, merchants and craftsmen, all of whom needed to be attracted from elsewhere to live in the embryonic settlement in order to build the place, service it and make it workable as a social unit. Accordingly Louis issued a Charter of Liberties offering attractive inducements to prospective newcomers. These included a variety of financial concessions—exemption from the customary taxes and tolls—as well as the promise of limited powers of self-government for the town, which was unusual in a medieval society in which communities tended to be yoked to feudal obligations of one kind or another.

More surprisingly the charter also offered moral safeguards designed to reassure potential citizens of the town that Aigues-Mortes would be a place of probity and law and order. This was to be no place for loose living. Adulterers were to be driven naked through the streets. It was not specified whether this punishment applied equally to men and women, though we do know that a later proviso stipulated that offenders should in future be lightly clad.

Little is known about which new buildings were constructed at this time in order to accommodate what would have been a rapid influx of inhabitants, but the housing programme must have been extensive as the fishing village became transformed within a few years into a garrison town. But at least we do know about the church, Notre-Dame des Sablons (Our Lady of the Sands), which still stands—another hefty slab of masonry close to the main square which today sports a somewhat coy nineteenth-century statue of King Louis in crusader outfit. (Artlovers may prefer Giotto's portrait of him in the church of S. Croce in Florence, painted not long after the king's death.) The church was substantially rebuilt at the time when Louis was preparing for the great crusade, and although it has been considerably altered over the following centuries its handsome Gothic nave must be much as it was when the king would have attended a farewell mass before taking to the sea. It may not bear comparison with Louis' other achievement in churchbuilding, the glorious Sainte-Chapelle in Paris; yet none the less it has a simplicity and dignity befitting the crusading venture which would have received its final blessing here.

But the most intimate link to Louis' presence in the town is a small early-Christian altar topped with a rough cap-stone which is known to have come from the abbey of Psalmodi. Its history is unclear, but speculation can hardly stray far from the truth: it may well have been a gift from the grateful abbot at the time when he was paying off the abbey's debts by selling Aigues-Mortes to the French monarch.

To assemble his crusading fleet Louis made ship-building contracts mainly with Genoa and Marseille, appointing two Genoese representatives to conduct the necessary negotiations on his behalf. The two men were officially described as "admirals", the first time such a title (Arabic in origin) was ever used in France. Besides the king, other lords who had "taken the cross" commissioned vessels of their own. One of these, the count of St. Pol, even ordered a ship to be built in Scotland, at Inverness. (What is more, it apparently arrived.) The king's own brother, Alphonse, who had become count of Toulouse following the disgrace of his predecessor for having supported the Cathars, commissioned a vessel from Brittany with the declared intention of accompanying the king to the Holy Land—which he never did, preferring to remain in France to help administer the country in his brother's absence. The largest ship to be built was named the *Paradise*, and it was equipped to carry a hundred horses below decks along with the knights who were to ride them and their servants. The same vessel was also designed to accommodate the king himself as well as the entire royal party, including Queen Marguerite, all of them provided with quarters in the raised "castles" fore and aft.

Then, as the ships arrived—after the inevitable delays—the "new town" of Aigues-Mortes found itself needing to accommodate in the region of five thousand soldiers along with their horses, servants, wives, concubines and sundry hangers-on. Many of the soldiers were hardened veterans of the Albigensian Crusade against the Cathars. Others were the customary adventurers and petty criminals, no doubt delighted to find themselves absolved by the church of all their crimes since they were now crusaders, and even more delighted since they were sanctioned to repeat those very crimes unchecked under the licence of a "holy war".

On the other hand, attractive though the forthcoming adventure may have seemed to the common soldiery, with overcrowding, disaffection, mosquitoes, disease, shortage of drinking-water and interminable months of waiting—much of it unpaid—only a painful exercise of the imagination can re-create what Aigues-Mortes must have been like during those early months of 1248.

Louis and his wife finally went on board the *Paradise* on Tuesday 25 August 1248. By now thirty-eight large ships were anchored at Aigues-Mortes in readiness. The entire crusading army proceeded to embark, including a small English contingent led by the Earl of

Salisbury, William Longsword. The fleet then waited for two days for a favourable wind. Supplies had already been sent ahead to Cyprus, which was safely under Christian rule, and where it was planned that the army would pass the coming winter.

The crusading fleet eventually set sail. From below the Tour de Constance it proceeded slowly down the narrow channel which ran westwards along the north side of what is now the Etang de la Marette and the Etang du Ponant, eventually reaching the sea at a point close to the present-day town of Le Grau-du-Roi. Louis' friend and biographer Jean de Joinville, who sailed with him, described the scene: "Soon the wind filled the sails and had taken us out of sight of land, so that we could see nothing but sky and water; and every day the wind took us further from the homes in which we were born."

The journey to Cyprus took the fleet three weeks. But King Louis himself would be away from home for six years. Accounts of his capture in Egypt, and of how his queen, Marguerite, negotiated his eventual released on payment of a huge ransom, lie outside the scope of a book on the Camargue, as does the story of the second crusade Louis undertook from Aigues-Mortes in 1279, and which claimed his life.

Louis' son, Philip III, succeeded him on the throne of France. And it is largely due to him that Aigues-Mortes became the startling medieval set-piece that we see today. Using income from taxes on merchant ships docking in the harbour, supplemented by a substantial contribution from a Genoese ship-owner and political leader Guglielmo Boccanegra, Philip undertook to reshape the town into a formal grid-pattern, which is still the geometry of the present town, with narrow streets crisscrossing at regular intervals. At the same time he enclosed the chequerboard of a town within a massive wall of stone, so creating a fortress more than a mile in circumference and guarded by no fewer than fifteen watchtowers. The ramparts are reckoned to have been completed within forty years, and the result remains one of the most awesome examples of medieval military architecture in Europe.

The subsequent history of Aigues-Mortes veers between the grim and the horrific. For all the fervour and bright hopes that had attended its beginnings, it is as though a curse fell on the town. By the time the great ramparts were completed early in the following century King Philip had been succeeded by his son, Philip IV, known as "the Fair". Within a few years the new French king, with the craven assistance of the first of the Avignon popes, Clement V, had succeeded in destroying the Knights Templar on the basis of trumped-up charges substantiated by confessions extracted under torture, in reality a pretext for destroying the Templars' power and grabbing their vast wealth. By one of the chilling ironies of history in which the Middle Ages abounds the Tour de Constance, which had been built by Philip's grandfather as a base from which to "liberate" the Holy Land, now became a prison for Templar knights whose order had been founded precisely to safeguard those same Christian lands in Palestine. Here, awaiting the stake or a lesser punishment if they were fortunate, they languished in the shadow of the very crusades they had been dedicated to defend. Gratitude was not a quality readily associated with King Philip the Fair.

No less unsavoury was an incident during the Hundred Years War between England and France a few decades later. In the aftermath of the Battle of Agincourt, with the English king Henry V now occupying the throne of France, a bitter conflict broke out between the supporters of the pro-English duke of Burgundy and those of the pro-French count of Armagnac. Aigues-Mortes, traditionally on the side of the Armagnacs, became drawn into this conflict when it was seized by the Burgundians in a surprise attack. The Armagnacs responded by besieging the place, and their supporters within the walls of the town succeeded in overpowering the garrison and opening the gates to the Armagnacs. The Burgundians were duly massacred in large numbers and their bodies piled up in one of the towers, then covered with salt to delay putrefaction until they could be buried. (It has to be said that of the many uses of the local industrial product, salt, this has to have been the most macabre.) Today, in commemoration of this ghoulish event, the site is still named the Tour des Bourguignons, or more graphically the Tower of the Salted Burgundians, and is the first of the fifteen defensive towers to be visited on an anti-clockwise circuit of the ramparts beginning at the Tour de Constance.

Events grew even worse in Aigues-Mortes as a result of the Wars of Religion, which tore France apart during the sixteenth century. In a rare exhibition of sectarian tolerance the French king, Henry IV, proclaimed an ending to the persecution of Protestant Huguenots by signing the Edict of Nantes in 1598, a gesture not unrelated to the fact that Henry had himself been a Protestant until converting to Catholicism in order to be acknowledged as king of France, uttering the famous words "Paris is worth a mass."

Less than a century later, and likewise politically motivated, Louis XIV decided to revoke the Edict of Nantes on the grounds that it had become redundant since all French Protestants had by now wisely converted to the "true faith". This was far from being the case, and one of the cities which still supported a sizable Protestant population was not far from Aigues-Mortes, namely Nîmes. Having enjoyed freedom of worship for almost a hundred years, the Protestants of Nîmes resented having that freedom arbitrarily withdrawn, and continued to hold their services, though for the most part discreetly and in secret. But as the authorities tightened their grip Protestant services became increasingly at risk, and in 1720 a secret prayer meeting of the Reformed Church of Nîmes held in a cave outside the city was interrupted by a band of soldiers who proceeded to arrest fifty men, women and children. After the trial—if that is not too generous a term—the pastor who had officiated at the prayer meeting was hanged, while fifteen of the male congregation were marched several hundred miles to the Atlantic port of La Rochelle from where they were dispatched to America. As for the women present at the meeting, they were condemned to prison with no prospect of release. And the prison in which they were incarcerated was none other than St. Louis' Tour de Constance in Aigues-Mortes.

Other Protestant women prisoners followed over the course of the next few years: probably as many as two hundred all told. We know the names of many of them, and we know a little about a few of them. Suzanne Mauran was five months pregnant when she was imprisoned in the Tour de Constance in 1730, and gave birth to a son there four months later. At least there would have been no shortage of midwives in the tower, though one shudders to think of the conditions in which the birth took place. Suzanne's mother-in-law is known to have sent her wooden planks for a bed so that she would not have to sleep on the bare stone floor. Nine years later her husband died. Finally, after three more years, she procured her release by agreeing to sign an "act of abjuration", formally renouncing her faith. A short time afterwards she married another Protestant.

Then there was Elizabeth Jullian, a married woman of twenty-nine with four children (whom she had to leave behind with her husband and in-laws). With her head shaved as a punishment for her faith she remained in the tower for twelve years until eventually agreeing to recant.

The Tour de Constance is today a shrine to these women. The building consists of just two rooms—or more accurately circular galleries—one above the other, with deep arrow-slit windows and lofty ceilings elegantly vaulted like inverted flowers. A modern plaque on the wall lists the names of twenty-five women imprisoned here. Neither Suzanne Mauran nor Elizabeth Jullian are among them, but the list does include the most celebrated of the tower's prisoners, a woman about whom much has been written, often casting her understandably enough as a feminist icon. She was Marie Durand, who was imprisoned in 1730 at the age of fifteen and not released for a further thirty-eight years until the prison was finally declared closed, by which time she was aged fifty-three. Scratched in the stone of the well in the centre of one of the rooms is the single word *Resister*, dialect for "Resist", which has long been attributed to the unyielding Marie Durand. There is no actual proof to support such a claim, yet it scarcely matters: whether she

The Tour de Constance, a shrine to Marie Durand and other Protestant women.

engraved the word or not, to have spent thirty-eight years of her life in prison when a simple renunciation would have obtained her release at any time must stand as one of history's most heroic testimonies to the unwavering power of faith.

A record survives of when the Tour de Constance was finally shut down as a prison. The task of releasing the prisoners and closing the place fell to a French aristocrat by the name of the Prince de Beauvau. The prince travelled to Aigues-Mortes in 1767 accompanied by his nephew, Stanislas-Jean de Boufflers, and it was he who has left us a harrowing account of their visit. He mentions no prisoners by name, but since Marie Durand was still a captive in the tower at the time she must have been one of the women he encountered.

"We found at the entrance of the tower," de Boufflers wrote, "an eager guard who led us through a dark and twisting passage and opened a great clanging door... I have no colours with which to paint the terrors of the picture which gradually grew upon our unaccustomed eyes. The scene was hideous yet pathetic, and interest in its victims struggled with disgust at their condition. Almost without air and light, fourteen women languished in misery and tears within that stone-walled chamber. As the commandant, who was visibly touched, entered the apartment, they all fell down together at his feet. I can still see them, bathed in tears, struggling to speak, unable at first to do anything but sob. Encouraged by our evident sympathy they all began to tell us their sorrows at once... The youngest of them was fifty, and she had been here since she was eight years old."

Whoever the nameless woman was, she had served a sentence even longer than Marie Durand.

De Boufflers' report is most readily available in a rich compendium of local history and folklore written by the High Victorian grandee Sir Theodore Andrea Cook, entitled *Old Provence*, first published in 1905 but recently reprinted. Cook's own acerbic footnote to de Boufflers' report deserves to be quoted here. He describes how he takes his own leave of the Tour de Constance, "which was built by the most saintly King of France, and that was put to such base uses by his successors; and it is significant that the swamps and deadly marshes of Aigues-Mortes should have been thus cleansed thirty years before the deluge of the Revolution cleansed the rest of France."

In August 1880, only a few years before Sir Theodore travelled here, a remarkable discovery was made which would still have been a talking-point in the town when he was conducting his own local researches. A stonemason who was engaged in restoring one of the arrow-slit windows of the Tour de Constance came across a bundle of coarse cloth which somehow had been hidden within the stonework. The bundle was found to contain items of clothing: two pairs of women's shoes, another pair that was clearly for a young girl, three pairs of children's slippers, plus some playing-cards, a pewter spoon and fragments of earthenware vessels. There was no clue to how they got there, or why they were hidden; none the less they came to light as a raw reminder of how even amid the cruelties of sectarian persecution the business of ordinary day-to-day life, grim and desperate though it was, somehow had to go on. There were children to be cared for, food somehow to be prepared, and endless hours to while away

Cook himself journeyed to Aigues-Mortes by train, noting on arrival that the smoke from the railway was "already blackening the ramparts of the crusaders." He was anything but attracted to the place, explaining gloomily that it was "surrounded by marshes that exhale perpetual ague" which contributed to "disease and desolation". As for the town itself, he found it to be "a withered chequerboard of haggard-looking streets", so much so that he shrank from actually sleeping in the town. Where he managed to find more agreeable accommodation among the disease-ridden marshes he omitted to inform his readers.

Sir Theodore was by no means the first writer to be drawn to the dark romance of this region of the Cathars, the crusades and the deadly wars of religion. A member of the French consular service by the name of Marie-Henri Beyle, better know as the novelist Stendhal, had come close to visiting Aigues-Mortes half a century earlier while on protracted leave from his official duties in Paris. Stendhal made the journey south between writing his two masterpieces, *Le Rouge et le Noir* (1830) and *La*

Chartreuse de Parme (1839), having planned a travel book which never saw the light of day in his lifetime. We do not know whether he seriously intended to visit Aigues-Mortes, though it is hard to believe that any travel-writer scouring the region for material in the Romantic era can have elected not to. In the event, the great man seems to have lost heart when he got as far as Nîmes, pronouncing with Parisian *hauteur* that "the stupidities of these provincials is beyond belief." Perhaps it is not surprising that the book never got to the printers.

Less than a decade after Stendhal's loss of heart a more vigorous student of romance managed to make it to Aigues-Mortes, and was alternately captivated and dismayed by what he discovered. He was Alexandre Dumas *père*. By this time, in the late 1840s, Dumas the Elder had already written a number of highly successful romantic novels including *The Three Musketeers* and *The Count of Monte Cristo*. Unfortunately the fame and wealth these rollicking stories brought him had fed his appetite for extravagant living to such an extent that he felt compelled to earn some quick money by travel-writing, then coming into vogue in Parisian literary circles, where well-to-do bourgeois who rarely travelled further than the Bois de Boulogne were beginning to enjoy the vicarious pleasure of reading about the peasantry and the primitive life. Dumas' travel journal, which he published in 1851, was entitled *Pictures of Travel in the South of France*. His "pictures" often failed to be quite as pretty as he would have liked; the Camargue in general (as described in Chapter 1) he found to be "an immense swamp... uninhabited and uninhabitable". The approach to Aigues-Mortes was not much better: "We soon found ourselves in an immense marsh, interspersed with large pools of water, in the centre of which were islands covered with weeds and shrubs." Then, "in the midst of these putrid marshes of France a poor habitation rises into view." This was Aigues-Mortes. When he finally reached the place he found it to be "a poor decayed city which is visited only by poets, historians and painters"—a revealing comment since it provides some of the earliest evidence we have of the growing romantic appeal of the town, in spite of the "deadly exhalations from all the surrounding swamps and marshes".

It is certainly true that by this time disease and commercial decline had taken its toll of Aigues-Mortes; the town was no longer a port of any importance except to fishermen, and the population of two to three thousand inhabitants was barely half the number who had lived there in its heyday.

On the other hand Dumas' eye was caught by several features of the place which lightened his gloom over the pervading decay, the swamps, the ferocious wind and the even more ferocious mosquitoes. He found much to admire in the sweeping triangular sails of the local fishing-boats as they set out to sea, a spectacle captured three decades later by Van Gogh in the paintings and drawings he executed at Les Saintes-Maries-de-la-Mer. Dumas also found his writer's imagination aroused by reminders of the town's heroic past. Aided no doubt by local guides keen to keep their famous visitor happy, he was overwhelmed to come across the carcass of what he was convinced was a crusading galley embedded at the water's edge. We have no idea if it was pointed out to him that a wooden vessel was unlikely to have survived in the mud for six hundred years, and what he came across was almost certainly a derelict fishing-boat. But Dumas was not to be put off by such mundane considerations. He was a great deal more sceptical, however, about the iron ring he was shown at the corner of the wall overlooking the former inner harbour, used—so he was informed by his enthusiastic guide—to tie up crusading vessels before their departure for the Holy Land. Dumas either knew, or had been informed, that the stone ramparts of Aigues-Mortes were not actually built until many decades after the crusading fleets had set sail.

It would be intriguing to know who Dumas had in mind when he claimed that the town was visited only by poets, historians and painters. To modern eyes the first artist of note to have worked at Aigues-Mortes was the young Frédéric Bazille almost two decades after Dumas' visit. Born in 1841, the son of a well-to-do Protestant dignitary in Montpellier, Bazille went to study painting in Paris and entered the studio of an eminent academician, Charles Gleyre, who had a reputation for being a lot less stuffy than his contemporaries in the artistic establishment. For this reason the place attracted young painters whose ambitions looked forward rather than back. Fellow students attending the Atelier Gleyre at this time included Claude Monet, Auguste Renoir and Alfred Sisley, with all of whom—Monet and Renoir in particular—Bazille formed a close friendship. They shared accommodation in Paris, with Bazille paying the lion's share, and they travelled and worked together with the intensity of pioneers. The four young students became the nucleus of what was to grow within a few years into the Impressionist Movement—though Bazille never lived even long enough to take part on the first Impressionist exhibition in Paris in 1874.

Being close to his home-town of Montpellier, Aigues-Mortes was a place Bazille was particularly anxious to visit. With its awesome ramparts and its dramatic setting in a wilderness of marshes it was a location that asked to be painted. Bazille first intended to travel there in 1866, but abandoned the idea due to an outbreak of cholera in the area. (One remembers Dumas' "deadly exhalations from the swamps and marshes".) Finally he made it in June the following year. "I have begun three or four canvases of the surroundings of Aigues-Mortes," he wrote. (Today one of these paintings hangs in the National Gallery in Washington, a second in the Metropolitan Museum, New York, while a third has remained in Montpellier, at the Musée Fabre.) Together they form among the most valuable record we have of what Aigues-Mortes looked like in the mid-nineteenth century before the town spilled out into the surrounding countryside and tourist coaches began to nudge up against the ancient walls.

In Bazille's paintings the massive ramparts stand out dramatically amid the creeks and marshy fields. Boats with the curving triangular sails which Dumas noticed are drawn up beneath the Tour de Constance. Horses graze in the shadow of the colossal gates. And where the modern road now leaps over the Canal du Rhône a cluster of thatched cottages such as Van Gogh was soon to draw in Les Saintes-Maries occupy the marshy space outside the walls. Also surviving from that brief visit in 1867 are delightful pencil sketches—some of them now in the Louvre, others in the Musée Fabre. They are precise and careful studies of what caught his eye: fishing-boats drawn up on the shore, houses crammed together behind the Tour de Constance, while others are of the vast sweep of ramparts which look as though they are ankle-deep in the surrounding waters.

There are only very few of them, alas. Bazille never had a chance to return. Three years later he volunteered for the French army during the Franco-Prussian War, and was killed in November 1870 by two bullets which struck him in his stomach. He was twenty-eight years old.

Nine or ten years after Bazille made his pictorial record of the town a literary heavyweight arrived in Aigues-Mortes. He was the American novelist Henry James, who had been living in Paris in the high-flying company of Gustave Flaubert, Ivan Turgenev, Emile Zola and Guy de Maupassant. Around 1876, before deciding to move more or less permanently to London, James began travelling in France, partly because it was a country that fascinated him, but also in order to gather material for the novels he was soon to write (notably *The Portrait of a Lady*), as well as to try his hand at the newly-fashionable genre of travelwriting. The result was *A Little Tour in France*, published a few years later in 1884.

James' account of his visit to Aigues-Mortes has a sharpness and a wit which make it refreshing reading after the narcissistic gloom of Dumas. Being an American intrigued by what he perceived to be the wisdom as well as the decadence of old Europe, he was more inclined than snooty Parisians to find a certain beauty and a certain dignity in a decaying city which possessed so rich a distant history—so much more distant than anything in his native country. He certainly approached the place in an optimistic state of mind. "It was my belief that Aigues-Mortes was a little gem," he wrote. He travelled by means of "a little, friendly, familiar, dawdling train," he explained. And he was not disappointed when he finally arrived: he found the town to be "the perfect thing of its kind in France". Admittedly the phrase "of its kind" suggested quite a few reservations. Aigues-Mortes clearly puzzled and amused him. He described it, somewhat quaintly, as like a billiard-table without pockets (presumably a reference to its rectangular lay-out), with an air of "bright, quiet melancholy". It is an apt phrase, and it is easy to picture the corpulent figure of James strolling round the dozing town at siesta-time, its "small stony whitewashed streets tenanted by a stray dog, a stray cat, a stray old woman... It can hardly be said to be alive... But if it is dead it has been very neatly embalmed," he added. He also noted "a very bad bronze statue of St. Louis" in the main square (not the last writer to offer such a judgment): in fact the statue was almost as bad in his eyes as the breakfast he had been served at the local inn, which had the nerve to bear the name of the sainted monarch who founded the town.

In short Henry James extracted a lot of fun out of Aigues-Mortes, and one wishes he could have devoted more space to sharing it with us.

The north side of the town, outside the walls, has been extensively built up in the century and a quarter since James' visit. As a result it comes as a delightful surprise—almost a shock—to follow the line of ramparts round to the south and east of the town and to find the long flank of medieval walls and watchtowers opening directly on to the water and the marshy fields exactly as it would have done in the late thirteenth century. Rarely can the old cliché "time stood still" feel more appropriate or truer.

Stretching southwards from the walled town the modern road leaps over what would have been the crusaders' inner harbour and heads straight for the coast, bisecting the lagoons and bypassing the extensive patchwork of salt-pans named after the Roman engineer Peccaius who established the salt industry here seventeen centuries ago. The road soon reaches the sea at the bustling port of Le Grau-du-Roi, named after the French king, St. Louis, whose crusading fleet departed—twice—from these shores. Not long ago Le Grau-du-Roi was just a busy fishing-port at the mouth of the Canal du Rhône. Today tourism has changed it profoundly, though not quite as much as it has its neighbouring clone, Port-Camargue, which exists purely to accommodate as many yachts as the giant marina can hold. Along this coast dazzling white apartment blocks rise along the waterfront in undulating shapes mimicking in a self-conscious fashion the sand-dunes and the glistening salt mountains which once dominated the lone fringes of this wilderness in the centuries before yachting marinas were invented.

But Le Grau-du-Roi, too, has its literary connection, of a heavy-weight kind as redoubtable as anything Aigues-Mortes can boast. In the years following the Second World War Ernest Hemingway spent a good deal of time in the Camargue and in Arles, indulging his passion for bull-fighting and for the company of bull-fighters, and by his brooding presence added yet another legend to a region already rich with them. Hemingway's novel *The Garden of Eden* is not one of his better-known works; it was still unpolished in manuscript form at the time of his suicide in 1961, and only published in New York twenty-six years later. Much of the book is set in Hemingway's beloved Spain, yet the story begins here, with his two lovers preparing to set out on their travels in search of an earthly paradise. "They were living at the Grau du Roi then" are the book's opening words, "and the hotel was on a canal that ran from the walled city of Aigues-Mortes across the low plain of the Camargue."

That low plain stretches eastwards from Le Grau-du-Roi. It is flooded intermittently by the old Roman salt-pans, as well as by a mosaic of lagoons whose surface is flecked with scarlet flamingos, and by meandering threads of water which were once rivulets of the fickle Rhône. Then, shortly before reaching the pilgrimage town of Les Saintes-Maries-de-la-Mer, a patch of that low plain is given over to something quite unexpected. It is the tomb of a man who, so the nearby inscription explains, "devoted his life to the traditions of the Camargue," and who more than any other figure in the history of this region can be said to personify its culture and its mystique.

He was Marquis Folco de Baroncelli-Javon, about whom it is necessary to say a great deal.

Chapter Seven

BLACK BULLS AND THE MARQUIS

In the centre of Les Saintes-Maries-de-la-Mer, a stone's-throw from the great gaunt church, stands a slender building which seems to be advancing towards you down the main street like the prow of an ocean liner. Emblazoned with heraldic crests and marble medallions, it was constructed in the nineteenth century in a vaguely classical style, and was originally intended to be the town hall. Then after the Second World War it became transformed into a museum of the Camargue, and was dedicated to the memory of a man who had recently died but who had lived in these marshlands for sixty years, in the course of which he did more to establish the identity and character of the Camargue than anyone in the history of the region. The museum duly bears his name; engraved above the entrance are the words: Musée Baroncelli.

If any man deserves to be described as the lord of the Camargue, then it is he: not least because he was in fact an aristocrat. His full name was Marquis Folco de Baroncelli-Javon.

The marquis' family background is colourful. The Baroncellis were wealthy and distinguished citizens of Florence. Early in the fourteenth century they were prestigious enough to commission a chapel in one of the most imposing churches in the city, S. Croce, decorating it with paintings long believed to be by Giotto, two of whose most celebrated fresco cycles are elsewhere in the same church, though the paintings in the Baroncelli chapel are most likely to be by his pupils. Shortly afterwards, probably during the later years of the Avignon papacy, a major branch of the family took advantage of the golden opportunities offered by the new seat of the papacy to establish a Florentine bank in the city. As a result the family prospered even more mightily, and chose to remain in Avignon even after the papacy returned to Rome in 1377.

From then onwards, though still owned by the Vatican, Avignon was placed in the hands of a series of papal legates, many of whom were just as absent as the popes themselves. Hence the city was actually run by administrators answerable to those legates who were themselves answerable to an absent pope. Towards the end of the fifteenth century one of these legates, Cardinal della Rovere (later to become Pope Julius II, patron of Raphael and Michelangelo), appointed the then head of the family, Pierre Baroncelli, to be the city's administrator. He was already one of Avignon's wealthiest citizens, and the family's growing prosperity was soon lavishly demonstrated by the construction of one of Avignon's finest Gothic mansions, known nowadays as the Palais du Roure.

The palace continued to be the Baroncelli family residence for the next four hundred years, and it was here that the future lord of the Camargue, Folco de Baroncelli, was born in 1869 and brought up.

However, there are curious twists to this story along the way. At least one branch of the Baroncelli family remained in Florence. In 1478, at about the time when Pierre Baroncelli was lording it in Avignon, a conspiracy was mounted in Florence against the ruling Medici family, culminating in a plot to murder the two Medici brothers, Giuliano and Lorenzo. Assassins duly struck during high mass in Florence's cathedral. Guiliano was killed outright; Lorenzo, though wounded in the neck, managed to escape. The culprits were caught and hanged, one of them being a certain Bernardo di Bandino Baroncelli, who, though executed, has survived as one of the most celebrated corpses in history.

The reason for such universal fame is that an artist who witnessed the hanging in the year 1479 was none other than Leonardo da Vinci, who proceeded to make a careful sketch of the corpse as it dangled from a window in what is now the Bargello Museum. In the margin of his sketch Leonardo even noted precisely what the dead man was wearing, concluding his list with the words "black shoes".

The Avignon branch of the Baroncelli family evidently remained untainted by these dark events in Florence, since half a century later Pope Leo X conferred the title of marquis on the head of the family in Avignon. The honour may seem the more surprising since Pope Leo was the son of Lorenzo the Magnificent, who as a young man had so narrowly escaped being murdered in the plot in which a member of the Baroncelli family had been implicated, and for which he had been publicly hanged.

There is one further twist in the tale. The title bestowed on Baroncelli was "Marquis of Javon", this being the name of a family property deep in the Vaucluse to the east of Avignon. The title survived over the following centuries even though at some stage the property itself passed out of the family's hands. Two centuries later the Château de Javon achieved a certain dark notoriety by being one of the possessions of another local marquis. He was the Marquis de Sade, and it would be hard indeed to imagine any figure, aristocratic or otherwise, less like Marquis Folco de Baroncelli-Javon.

In the mid-nineteenth century the Baroncellis had made available their family home in Avignon, the Palais du Roure, to a group of young writers who were dedicated to the revival of Provençal culture and in particular its traditional language known as Occitan. (The Palais du Roure was so-named by Frédéric Mistral, *roure* meaning "oak", a term he awarded to the most faithful members of the Félibrige group who regularly gathered round him in the Baroncelli palace, reading their works and planning the great Provencal cultural renaissance.) Mistral, the Félibrige's leader, had by now already begun work on his epic poem *Mirèio*, which was soon to win him iconic status in Provence and fame worldwide.

The young Folco de Baroncelli grew up within the euphoric glow of this idealistic coterie. Then, when he was twenty-two he was offered the post of assistant editor of a periodical in the Provençal language entitled *Aïoli*, which Mistral had just founded. As the poet's loyal protégé Baroncelli was fiercely dedicated to the Provençal cause. But at the same time his deepest passions lay far outside the literary hothouse of the Félibrige meetings with their nostalgia for the troubadours and their dreams of a reborn Occitania. Baroncelli had discovered the Camargue. Precisely why he should have been drawn to the wilderness after an urban youth spent in an Avignon palace among men of letters is unclear. Doubtless by this time he had become thoroughly steeped in the mystique surrounding the writings of his mentor, Mistral, and in particular the maestro's by-now-legendary *Mirèio*, which of course was set romantically in the Camargue.

Hence proof-reading and negotiating with Avignon printers began to occupy a good deal less of his time than the rural way of life in the marshlands of the Rhône delta. And soon he decided to leave Avignon, using the Baroncelli mansion only as an occasional base. He settled permanently in the depths of the Camargue, enjoying a primitive style of living that could hardly have differed more radically from life in the family palace. Yet the magnetism of this new environment was not so much the romantic appeal of an untamed landscape, or even the simple lifestyle of its inhabitants; it was the irresistible attraction to him of the race of black bulls which roamed there, and which he perceived to be in danger of dying out—at least as a pure race. As Frédéric Mistral was soon to write of him a little regretfully, "The wretch has completely lost his mind over bulls."

Baroncelli set out to be a breeder of Camargue black bulls.

At the same time his own literary efforts were running parallel to his new vocation—as they were always to do. His first volume of verse, *Blad de Luno* (Corn of the Moon) was a celebration of traditional life in the delta which centred on the breeding and welfare of Camargue bulls and wild horses.

It was a Spartan existence. Life in a primitive farmhouse amid the swamps and the mosquitoes offered few creature comforts. There was no electricity, no running water and only the most primitive of domestic facilities of any kind. If this may have seemed to others to be going a little too far "back to nature", there was never any question about his commitment to the venture. It was to be his chosen way of life, but also a grand plan which included those around him. There is an endearing tale relating to his marriage, which took place in 1894, when Baroncelli was twenty-five. His bride-to-be was a Parisian lady from a background of well-to-do bourgeoisie. Her parents, doubtless impressed by their future son-in-law's aristocratic credentials, arranged (and doubtless paid for) a honeymoon for the young couple in places they deemed fit to receive the young marquis and his marchioness, namely Nice, Monte Carlo, Capri and Sorrento. Young Folco had other ideas. After the ceremony in Paris the journey south was naturally by train. But in the course of its leisurely progress towards the Riviera the train stopped briefly at Arles, whereupon Baroncelli is said to have turned to his bride with the suggestion, "Shall we dismount?" No doubt mystified, she none the less agreed. The couple proceeded to spend their honeymoon, and the next five years of their life together, in the primitive reed-thatched *cabane*, interspersed with regular visits to the family palace in Avignon. There is no record of how his Parisian in-laws reacted to their daughter's change of lifestyle, or whether the subsequent arrival of three granddaughters over the next few years softened whatever dismay they may have experienced.

In time, however, his wife came to spend most of the year in Avignon, partly no doubt in the interests of her three girls, but also perhaps for the sake of her own sanity. Being stuck in the middle of the marshes with three daughters, few luxuries and few friends can hardly have been the life of her dreams, however devoted she may have been to her marquis. Then, five years after their marriage Baroncelli arranged with the owner of a local farmhouse, the Mas de l'Amarée, to take over the place and be in charge of its herd of two hundred bulls and fifty horses. The house was close to Les Saintes-Maries, but it still had no electricity or running water, in common with most country dwellings at this time. Baroncelli had now become a stock-breeder—a *manadier* (a *manade* being the local term for an estate on which animals were bred and reared).

From now on this was to be his life, interspersed with writing poetry. The two activities dovetailed perfectly. The daylight hours were devoted to his animals; the lamp-lit evenings to writing about his experiences of a life devoted to this wild place. Transport was of course on horseback: a *manadier* more or less lived on a horse, there being no other local transport except for the little train which at that time trundled from Arles to Les Saintes-Marie. Baroncelli would regularly ride the fifty miles to Avignon in order to see his wife and children, and then ride back again. The iron ring to which he attached his horse still protrudes from a wall opposite the Palais du Roure.

Unfortunately there was little money to be made from raising bulls. Soon the life of a rural *manadier* began to prove incompatible with maintaining a palace in the former papal city. And in 1909 he felt compelled to sell it, though retaining an apartment where his family continued to live, and where he could continue to ride the fifty miles to visit them.

Baroncelli's dedication to his work in the Camargue was lifelong and unwavering. It can seem obsessive, and perhaps it was; if so, it was an obsession born of love and unswerving determination. It had the strength of a religious faith, and the nature of that faith was well expressed by Frédéric Mistral in his old age, when he urged Baroncelli to create an "open-air museum" which would be consecrated to "preserving the purity of the race of bulls… and which shall be the living complement to my museum" (i.e. the Musée Arlaten in Arles).

Mistral as usual was being prophetic. But whereas many of the poet's prophesies relating to Occitania seem directed towards Utopia, the vision of an open-air museum in the Camargue which he offered to Baroncelli was, as it turned out, both plausible and realistic. A museum, for Mistral, was not something dead, a nostalgic memorial to a vanished past. It was a place where living and lasting values could be displayed and flourish, in defiance of materialistic forces which sought to corrupt and destroy those values. In this connection Mistral was a precursor of those who champion "green" issues today, who enable conservation areas and wildlife parks to be established, and even those who make nature documentaries for television.

If it was Mistral who had the dream, his vision of an open-air museum in the Rhône delta was given a practical framework by Folco de Baroncelli several years after Mistral's death. It was in 1922 that he called for a national park to be created in the Camargue. And his appeal was backed by a compelling argument which was decades ahead of its time.

> We classify ancient stones, arenas, palaces, ramparts and cathedrals as historic monuments so that no one can destroy them. Is Nature... not just as much a precious historic monument, which none the less could soon be destroyed by what we call civilization?

It was a pioneering statement. The view that areas of the natural world may be as valuable a part of our cultural heritage as buildings was all but revolutionary at that time, and Baroncelli is too rarely given due credit—perhaps because some of his other statements relating to the Camargue verge on the fanciful. Almost fifty years later his vision became a reality when the entire delta between the Grand and Petit Rhône was declared a Regional National Park, within which lie many of the Camargue's numerous nature reserves today, in particular the Réserve Nationale de Camargue centring on the huge lagoon that is more like an inland sea: the Vaccarès.

The principal focus of Baroncelli's working life during the sixty years he lived in the delta was that majestic, almost godlike creature, the

Camargue black bull. And it was to a great extent the marquis' doing that this noble animal has come to symbolize the Camargue itself. By his efforts Baroncelli endowed it with a certain aura, an irresistible mystique. Fortunately there was plenty of material from which he was able to cultivate that mystique. Here was a creature whose origins were shrouded in the myths of pre-history, some of them romantic, some of them religious, many of them speculative, but all of them intriguing.

To begin with, there is one distinctive difference between the Spanish bull of the *corrida* (bullfight) and the bull of the Camargue. The former has horns protruding forward, the better to gore you with, while the horns of the Camargue bull rise elegantly upwards in the shape of a lyre. Since Babylonian times at least bulls have been held in special reverence in a variety of cultures, whether occupying a special place in the celestial zodiac (Taurus) or worshipped as a god in countless mythologies and religious practices. It can be no coincidence that speculation over the origin of the Camargue race of bull should have been fuelled by the evidence of many of the earliest-known images of bulls, which show the creature bearing lyre-shaped horns rather than horns which protrude forward.

Two of the most celebrated of these early bull images, both from the second millennium BC, are the magnificent *rhyton* (a ceremonial drinking vessel) from Minoan Crete in the shape a black bull's head with golden horns found in the palace of Knossos and now displayed in the Archaeological Museum in Herakleion; the second being a similar silver and gold *rhyton* of a bull's head found at Mycenae, and now in the Greek National Museum in Athens. Both images show the lyre-shaped horns of the Camargue bull. More than ten thousand years earlier still, the Stone Age cave paintings at Lascaux, in central France, includes similar representations of raised horns in the famous Hall of the Bulls. Also in France, in the heart of in the Maritime Alps, one of Europe's most unforgettable walks leads you to a height of almost ten thousand feet along the rough flank of Mont Bégo to where some forty thousand Bronze Age (and later) images have been stippled on slabs of bare limestone scattered across an area called appropriately the Vallée des

Merveilles. *Bégo* itself means "home of the bull god", and the god's revered image is present everywhere in this bleak wilderness, once again in the form of lyre-shaped horns.

Perhaps too much can be made of the coincidence of the shape of a bull's horns. None the less it does provide a certain spiritual ancestry spread over a vast span of time and diversity of cultures, which must go a long way towards explaining the mystical cult of the Camargue bull, and why to people like Folco de Baroncelli the creature came to acquire an almost supernatural status. Whatever else may be true, from the shape of those horns alone the black bulls of the Camargue clearly descend from some prehistoric race. Baroncelli believed that this race must have originated in Asia, perhaps in Persia or the Indian subcontinent, and that after the Ice Age they gradually made their way westwards into the Mediterranean lands and southern Europe as the climate warmed—doubtless arousing fear and wonder by their formidable bearing and physical strength, and hence becoming worshipped as deities.

One of the earliest surviving reports of bulls in the Camargue was written in the sixteenth century by a visiting lord from Arles by the name of Pierre Quiqueran de Beaujeu, who set about making a chronicle of daily life during his travels in Provence which he called *Provence Loué* (perhaps best rendered as "In Praise of Provence"), so becoming a travel writer centuries before such an occupation became fashionable. He recorded that there were sixteen thousand bulls in the Camargue at this time; presumably they were bred for meat. "Just as their numbers are large," Beaujeu added, "so is their temper." Even allowing for exaggeration by local breeders keen to impress their noble visitor the number is still surprisingly high—roughly equal to the number today—especially as most of the large farmhouses of the *manadiers* which are now scattered across the Camargue were not built until at least a century later. Clearly the beef industry was flourishing a great deal earlier than it is sometimes assumed. These high numbers appear to have been maintained, and even increased, over the following centuries: certainly there is no record of any dramatic decline.

Disaster only struck during the Second World War, when food shortages led to bulls being systematically shot. The situation worsened when the threat of allied invasions caused the Germans to roll over Pétain's Vichy government and occupy the south. The bulls were now ruthlessly slaughtered by a hungry occupying force. Marshal Goering made matters worse by commandeering fifty of the surviving animals with a view to breeding them in Germany—an enterprise which came to nothing, or most likely ended up on grateful Berlin dinner-tables. Soon only one hundred and seventy adult bulls remained in the Camargue, and by the end of the war the number had shrunk to a mere thirty-seven.

Baroncelli himself never lived to see the post-war revival which rescued the race from extinction, having died during the Second World War shortly after the German invasion of the south (about which more later). Yet his legacy was the collective resolve among the *manadiers* to set about building up the numbers of the Camargue bull by careful and selective breeding from the small surviving stock.

During his lifetime the marquis is said to have been regarded by those who worked with him as the greatest expert on the Camargue bull that the region had ever known. For more than half a century he had presided over every aspect of the animals' life and welfare; and since a bull may live as long as thirty or even forty years there would have been a great many animals he had known and worked with all their lives. He would have been familiar year after year with the four- or five-day trek northwards on horseback driving the bulls to their summer pasture, and equally familiar with the festival surrounding the annual ceremony of the *ferrade*, the branding of young bulls with the emblem of their particular *manade*.

Above all he was passionately involved in the celebrated *course libre*, the Camargue "bull games". In fact he was largely responsible for re-viving them, though sceptical voices have claimed that he actually invented them. Whatever the true origin of these bull games, the *course libre* is conducted in every arena in the region today, and occupies a unique place at the heart of the Camargue's popular culture.

The essential difference between the *course libre* and the Spanish-style bullfight is that in the latter the bull is killed, while in the former he is not: he is merely teased and thoroughly infuriated, As a result, anyone who has ever watched these bull games in the arenas of the Camargue and the surrounding area will appreciate that a bull's' survival, and hence his ability to come back for more next time, makes him the more canny and certainly more dangerous. As Lawrence Durrell observed in *Caesar's Vast Ghost* (1990):

> Though the black fighting bulls of the Camargue are small, they wear a large and deadly crown of horns. Moreover they have seen the man and studied his ways on the range long before they find themselves face to face with him in the ring. And they are cunning as dogs… After every fight he is decanted back on the range. In a very short time a valiant small bull, realising that he is not going to be killed, but simply played for his cockade, will become a seasoned and cunning adversary.

The white-clad men who engage in these bull games may not be dressed up in the gorgeous *macho* costume of a Spanish matador, largely because they need to be more nimble than any matador. The bulls know the

rules of these games as well as they do.

In short, the object of the Camargue bull game is for a group of players, called *razeteurs*, armed only with a metal comb (a *razet*) to be sharp enough to snatch a red *cocarde*, or rosette, which has been placed in just about the most dangerous place possible, on the bull's forehead between his horns. If one of the *razeteurs* succeeds in this mission, then he or one of his team-mates will try to remove one of two tassels which have been attached to the horns themselves. Each trophy comes with prize money, and this is announced by sponsors, or sometimes spontaneously by enthusiastic spectators. Needless to say the bull is rarely co-operative in these ventures, and there are numerous postcards on sale outside the arena for the enjoyment of tourists depicting *razeteurs* desperately leaping the protective barrier, or being propelled over it by those lyre-shaped horns.

Vincent Van Gogh, during his stay in Arles, attended one of these events in April 1886, and described the occasion in a letter to his brother Theo in Paris. "Yesterday I saw another bull fight, where five men played the bull with darts and cockades. One toreador crushed a testicle jumping the barricade. He was a fair man with grey eyes and plenty of sang-froid: people say he'll be ill a long time. He was dressed in sky-blue and gold."

The bulls themselves that take part in these frolics are known as *cocardiers*, and one of the most famous of them, by the name of Lou Vovo, was bred by the marquis himself. But the most highly esteemed of them all was a *cocardier* called Le (or *Lou* in Provençal) Sanglier—meaning rather puzzlingly "the wild boar"—which took part in no fewer than sixty displays of *course libre* between the year 1919 and 1930. The bull's fame is now enshrined in the form of a monument, complete with portrait and inscription in Provençal, marking the fiftieth anniversary of the animal's death and erected close to the village of Le Cailar north-west of the Camargue, where the bulls would often be driven for their summer pasture.

Preceding the bull games is an event which can often be more dramatic and certainly more alarming than the games themselves. This is the *abrivado*, which is the free running of the bulls through the streets of whatever town is holding the event. The occasion is not unlike the famous running of the bulls through the streets of Pamplona, except that these Camargue bulls, unlike their Spanish counterparts, have been here many times before and therefore know precisely where and how to cause the maximum panic. One of the most colourful accounts of an . *abrivado* appears in the autobiography of the South African poet Roy Campbell, *Light on a Dark Horse* (1952). Campbell lived and worked in the Camargue for some years during the 1920s and 1930s, earning a precarious living as a fisherman and as an apparently successful *razeteur*.

> At dawn the young men ride away to spy out the cattle on their pastures, and when they have rounded up the required number get them moving in the same direction quietly towards the town. As they near the town they goad the bulls to a trot, accelerating when they come near the main street, until a torrent of bulls and horses thunders in among the cafes and shops, the bulls hitting the ground with all four feet together and making the earth fly beneath them, and tremble, and resound; and the horses behind them going hell-for-leather, with the riders yelling for all they're worth, and the citizens, and other pedestrians and poultry stampeding for the doors, and the boldest ones waiting till the very last second till they slam the door. Shotguns, petards, and rockets are fired from the crowded windows, bands play, drums are rattled, and tin cans beaten as if to scare away all the locust plagues of Egypt. The uproar is so terrific that the bulls hardly know if they're going or coming; sometimes they rush down side streets, try to jump through doors or windows, or into backyards only to be chased after by some of the riders and driven back to the main route, where they are finally driven through a circle of carts chained together in the central square of the town, into the corral which awaits them; or into the arena itself, if the town happens to have one.

Campbell's relish at the bedlam caused by rampaging bulls then takes a prurient turn when he goes on to describe the events which accompany the *abrivado*. What happens is "related to prehistoric fertility rites," he claims solemnly. The biggest and strongest bull is lassoed and led through the streets, "and all the girls who are brave enough try to get in behind him and touch his testicles in the hope that it will confer fertility upon them to bear many strapping sons and strapping daughters"—an observation which may seem to speak more for the masculine posturing of the author than it does for the dreams of Camargue maidens.

Displays of the *course libre* generally take place in the smaller arenas scattered about the region. But they also regularly feature as part of the folklore festivals held in the Roman amphitheatres of Arles and Nîmes. These areas are normally the venue for the annual summer *feria* with its Spanish-style *corrida* in which the bull (a quite different breed from the Camargue bull) is ritually killed by the matador's rapier. Yet the *corrida*, like the Spanish bull itself, is a relatively recent import to Provence. The massive Roman amphitheatres constructed in the first century AD, not long after the Colosseum in Rome, and capable of seating 25,000 people, were designed originally for the Romans' favourite gladiatorial contests and blood-sports involving wild animals and hapless Christians.

These gruesome displays continued long after Christians were spared being devoured by lions, and it appears from the few records we have that at some stage bulls may have taken the place of Christians—with far more successful results. In his memoirs a certain Bernard Boisset recounts an event which took place in the year 1402 when the French king (it would have been Charles the Mad, whose knights were later mown down at Agincourt) was treated to a contest in the amphitheatre at Arles between a lion and a bull, which the bull won. A century and a half later, another king of France, Charles IX, the feeble son of Catherine de Medicis, was honoured with a similar contest, again resulting in victory for the bull, which on this occasion we know to have been a Camargue bull.

The present-day bull games can seem playful compared to the bloodbaths of old. Yet the most significant change is the emphasis on skill and human agility which the *course libre* demands. It is for this reason above all that historians of Provençal culture have sought to establish a link between the Camargue bull games and early ceremonies in which athletes and bulls engaged in ritual games. The most tempting of such links is with the spectacular bull-leaping sport vividly described on painted murals and an ivory figurine found by the British archaeologist Sir Arthur Evens at the Minoan palace of Knossos in Crete, all dating from the second millennium BC. This link is strengthened in the eye of the beholder by the similarity (mentioned earlier in this chapter) between the lyre-shaped horns of Minoan bulls and those of the Camargue race of today. Nothing would have given Baroncelli greater pleasure than to be assured that his beloved Camargue bulls were the direct descendants of the Cretan bull—whose capture, after all, was one of the Seven Labours of Hercules. Alas, there is not one shred of evidence to suggest any connection between the antics of bull-leaping Minoans and those of the modern *razeteur*, even if a similar race of bulls should be common to both sports.

The marquis himself was convinced that the origin of the Camargue bull games lay deep in early religious practices in Asia relating to the Persian god of the sun and of fire, Mithra. Here at least there was a plausible historical link with the contemporary Camargue. The cult of Mithra is believed to have been brought to Europe as a result of the Greek conquests in Iran by Alexander the Great. Mithraism was then adopted by the Romans, who were expert at borrowing other peoples' gods, and in consequence spread throughout much of the Roman Empire. The second link in the chain was, of course, Julius Caesar's establishment of Roman Provence (*Provincia*), bringing with him the worship of Mithras (as the god was now called) and therefore the worship of the bull. Precisely how Mithraic bull worship may be reconciled with the taunting and mockery of the bulls by *razeteurs* in the Provençal arenas could be explained, even if tenuously, by the existence in Mithraic caves of frescoes representing the ritual sacrifice of the bull-god: in other words the *razeteur* plucking the red rosette from the bull's forehead is really performing a symbolic sacrifice of the sacred creature—or so the argument runs.

Baroncelli did his best to convince those around him of this link with pre-Christian rituals. He even proposed celebrating the centenary of Frédéric Mistral's birth in 1930 by sacrificing a bull on the altar in the crypt of the church at Les Saintes-Maries-de-la-Mer on the ground that the altar in question was believed to be of Mithraic origin. Needless to say the local priests took a different view of the proposition, even threatening the marquis with excommunication if he were to persist in this pagan enterprise.

Baroncelli received a further setback in his quest for the historical roots of the Camargue bull games when he claimed that they had been keenly watched by popes and members of the papal court during the "exile" years of the fourteenth century when the seat of the papacy was in Avignon. The marquis' assertion was briskly contradicted by the curator of the Palais des Papes on the grounds that there was no evidence whatever for such a claim. In fact there was some suspicion that, far from the bull games being a revived tradition, there was actually no tradition at all, and they were to a large extent a modern creation, a view expanded recently by a American academic, Robert Zaretsky of the University of Houston, in his book *Cock and Bull Stories* in which he claims that the Camargue's "humid air and isolation made it a hothouse for the orchids of invented traditions."

If the Camargue bull games really do represent an "invented tradition", then the invention cannot be laid at Baroncelli's door. Van Gogh's description of a contest which is clearly the modern *course libre* was of an event which took place in 1886, when the marquis was still a youth, and four years before he settled in the Camargue. The only marked difference between the performance Van Gogh witnessed and those of today lies in the clothing of the *razeteurs*. The painter described his contestants as "toreadors" who were clothed "in sky-blue and gold": in other words they were still dressed as if they were participants in a Spanish bullfight. What Baroncelli seems to have done was simply to swap the traditional Spanish bullfighter's costume for the plain white outfit and black beret of the modern *razeteur*. In doing so he gave the *course libre* a distinctive local flavour. Besides, as we shall see later, Baroncelli loved inventing uniforms.

Not all traditions are necessarily very old. Musicologists may tell you that the Scots were about the last people in Europe to adopt the bagpipe. And the "traditional" Spanish bullfight as we know it dates back no further than the eighteenth century. Traditions answer present needs as often as they do the voices of history. Baroncelli's orchestration of the Camargue games appears to have answered just such a requirement; a need among the people of the south to establish a culture that would pull together so many elements in this region—a region which was overflowing with history but had somehow never achieved an identity, having been for so long overshadowed, and in a sense crushed, by the weight and authority of France. This was one of Baroncelli's outstanding achievements, as to some extent it was also Mistral's. Together they gave the region a face, a personality, a mystique, a certain glamour.

It was to prove highly seductive, highly infectious, and above all masculine. Like Ernest Hemingway, like the French novelist and dramatist Henry de Montherlant, the poet Roy Campbell was another of those testosterone-fuelled writers to be drawn to the Camargue by the allure of the mystique which Mistral and Baroncelli had done so much to create. And they in turn contributed much to that glamour. Bulls symbolized the maleness they all cultivated. But whereas Hemingway and de Montherlant were content to be spectators in these male sports, Campbell throw himself enthusiastically into the ring. He became a celebrated *razeteur*.

Campbell's laconic words are an appropriate footnote to the story of the Camargue bull games. "I did a lot of bull-fighting at this time," he wrote in his autobiography, "but lived extravagantly in excess of my winnings." However, he added, the bribes he received for losing well exceeded whatever he got for winning. He could then go fishing and with luck catch a "scarlet sea-scorpion known as a *rascasse* which is the principal necessity for a bouillabaisse." But first, he explained, you needed to "trim sixteen or seventeen venomous fangs," a single sting from which "will make you sick for a week."

He might well have echoed an earlier romantic writer who had also fallen for the mystique of the Camargue. For Alexandre Dumas, *bouillabaisse*, the legendary fish stew from Marseille, was quite simply "the result of the most advanced state of culinary civilization". It was, he added, "Homeric". And no accolade could be more appropriate to the dreams and aspirations of Mistral and Baroncelli.

Chapter Eight

WHITE HORSES OF THE SEA

Perhaps the most enduring image of the Camargue is of a herd of white horses prancing across the shallows of a lagoon in the evening sunlight, their heads raised, manes flying, tails sweeping the surface of the water, their hooves sending up a thousand pearls of spray.

They are the spirit of the marshes, the emblem of the marshes, the romance of the marshes.

If legend is to be believed, they have always been here, or at least long before human beings settled in the delta. Certainly they are perfectly adapted to this place as though nowhere else could have suited them so well. They are just as much at home in water as they are on land. Their hooves are broad and tough enough to have no need to be shod. They are blessed with remarkable stamina, and they are hardy enough to be impervious to the extremes of temperature which the Camargue endures. They flourish though they spend most of their lives virtually in the wild, surviving even when the surrounding lagoons freeze over and the ice needs to be broken for them to drink. A certain native bloody-mindedness seems to carry them through. Probably no other race of horse could stand such conditions; indeed different breeds have been introduced from time to time as an experiment, and have failed to survive. It has even been claimed—though the evidence is unconvincing—that Camargue horses can see just as well by night as by day.

Traditionally their only large predator was the wolf. But these had been hunted to death by the mid-nineteenth century; a tiny islet to the south of the Vaccarès is still called the Radeau du Loup, possibly where the last wolf was shot. On the other hand there are smaller predators, and these do exist in vast numbers: ticks, leeches, midges, horseflies and the harmless-looking little *arabies*, which visiting Americans have been heard to call "no-see-ums" as they ruefully dab sting relief on reddened faces and arms. Then of course there are the mosquitoes. No fewer than twenty-four species of mosquito breed in the Camargue, a statistic not boldly advertised in the tourist offices in Arles, Aigues-Mortes or Les Saintes-Maries-de-la-Mer. Yet from the point of view of the Camargue horses themselves, one of the most salutary results of climate change has come to their aid in recent years: this is the arrival from southern Spain of that cousin of the local White Egret, the Cattle Egret, as a resident breeding species. True to their name, these robust birds find a ready larder of nourishment in the form of parasitic insects as they perch on the backs of horses grazing in the fields—a practice much to the relief of the horses themselves and to the delight of tourists wielding digital cameras.

Poets have long extolled the virtues and the beauty of Camargue horses. In Frédéric Mistral's epic poem *Mirèio* they are described as having "manes like the waves of the sea". The Marquis Baroncelli, who rode these horses all his life, used them as his regular means of transport to Avignon and back to visit his family. On one occasion, in the company of the mayor of Les Saintes-Maries-de-la-Mer, the marquis rode all the way to Lyon and back in forty-three hours—a journey not far short of three hundred miles.

Today there are in the region of three thousand horses roaming the Camargue, nearly all of then in small herds of about fifteen mares, selected stallions being let loose among them in the breeding season. They are rarely stabled, or hand-fed. The mares live in the wild, and are only occasionally saddled or ridden. The stallions join them to mate in the spring and early summer, and the females give birth in the open without assistance or human presence.

The traditional role of the Camargue horses is to guard and round up the bulls, though with the advance of tourism they have increasingly become vehicles for horse-trekking in the marshes—the ubiquitous *promenade à cheval* which has become one of the major industries of the delta.

They have also come to perform an important ceremonial role, both in the folkloric festivals that take place in the Roman arenas of Arles and Nîmes, and in particular in the annual ceremony held in Les Saintes-Maries-de-la-Mer (described in Chapter 2) when the images of the Two Marys and the gypsy "queen" Sara are led back into the sea from where they came, accompanied by their escort of white horses and mounted *gardians* in their distinctive garb and brandishing their long slender tridents.

Uniforms help establish a certain group personality, and like the Canadian "Mountie" and the Mid-West cowboy, the Camargue *gardian* has become something of a local icon and an essential ingredient of the region's mystique. The fraternity to which the *gardians* belong dates from early in the sixteenth century: 2 January 1512 saw the foundation in Arles of the Confrérie des Gardians de Taureaux et de Chevaux de Camargue. The ceremony took place in the church dedicated to St. George, who became their patron saint, and who still features on the *gardians'* traditional flag. They carry the flag on ceremonial occasions, and it shows the saint riding his Camargue horse, from where he expertly spears the dragon which was about to devour the legendary maiden—all of which contributes towards making the *gardian* something of a heroic figure.

More recently, in 1907, Marquis Baroncelli introduced a further organization more suited to the regional sentiments of the day, in which the *gardians* became identified as belonging to the *Nacioun gardiano*. Each year since that date, on whatever Sunday is closest to St. George's Day (23 April), they assemble on their white horses in full regalia on the broad Boulevard des Lices in Arles, before processing through the narrow streets of the old town and into the Roman amphitheatre. After a formal reception here the mounted *gardians* make their way a short distance to the medieval church of Notre-Dame-de-la-Major, which stands high above the old city ramparts; and here they dismount and attend a solemn mass with hymns sung, of course, in Provençal. It is among the most colourful and stirring days of the Provençal calendar.

One of the obligations required of members of the *Nacioun gardiano* was that on such ceremonial occasions they should wear the prescribed costume of their fraternity. This consists of a purple or bright-coloured cotton shirt printed with local Provençal motifs, a black velvet jacket lined with red or grey silk, pale moleskin trousers with dark piping, and finally a black broad-brimmed hat. There existed no tradition of any such uniform for the *gardians*, splendid and authentic though they certainly appear when they wearing it, and it may come as no surprise to learn that it was Baroncelli himself who designed it. One item of clothing that was traditionally local was the hat; this was based on a style frequently worn by horsemen in the neighbourhood of Lunel, a small town a little to the north of the Camargue. The marquis discovered where such hats were still being made, and proceeded to place an order for them to be distributed among his fellow *gardians*—and which he paid for himself.

The gardians' costume was now complete. "And thus a myth was born," wrote the historian and authority on the region, Sophie Delavoie, in her introduction to a wonderfully illustrated book entitled *Horses of the Camargue*.

A similar mystique has become attached to the *gardian's* picturesque white *cabane*, so vividly caught by Vincent Van Gogh in several drawings he made during his stay in Les Saintes-Maries-de-la-Mer in the spring of 1888, a number of which are still dotted here and there across the marshes. Traditionally they were used by stockmen, hunters and fishermen, as well as by *gardians*, their function being to provide temporary accommodation and shelter mostly between spring and autumn or whenever people needed to be in the open Camargue for tending animals or shooting duck, which arrive in vast numbers on migration. The *cabanes* were built of mud-bricks and thatched with overlapping layers of the local tall reeds known as *sagno*, which was harvested each autumn. The buildings were positioned very carefully to take account of the extreme weather conditions prevailing in the delta, especially the mistral, which regularly savages the Camargue as well as much of Provence, bending trees, whipping up both sand and water, and driving any sane human being safely indoors. Accordingly the rounded end of the building is the one facing north and without windows, hunching its shoulders against the onslaught of the mistral, whereas the entrance is at the southern end, sheltered and welcoming the sun. (The word *mistral*, incidentally, bears no relation to the poet Frédéric Mistral, except linguistically. They share a common origin in the Latin *magister*, meaning "master", a word that none the less seems entirely appropriate to both the wind and the poet.)

Today the authentic *cabanes* are far outnumbered by a rash of imitations. The little railway station at Méjanes, serving a tourist train service, is built in the style of one. Elsewhere they cluster like outsize bee-hives among the sprawling outskirts of Les Saintes-Maries-de-la-Mer, serving as folkloric hotel accommodation—and, it has to be admitted, extremely attractive they are, both to look at and to stay in. They are approached by tiny bridges over streams and little ponds where marsh frogs croak energetically in the dusk and white egrets silently stalk the pools just outside your window at first light. They possess the saccharine charm of kitsch. And like toy-town model villages in the English Cotswolds they create a Lilliputian world—one that mirrors in miniature the wider Camargue beyond.

The origin of the white horses of the Camargue has exercised the imagination of enthusiasts as long as that of the region's legendary black bulls. The two share an enticing ancestry of myth. The mystery of where the horses came from is part of the mystique of the delta. There are a number of theories, varying from the romantic and speculative to the scientific and pseudo-scientific, and any attempt to steer a path through such a maze of conjecture can feel like a journey without maps. All the same it is intriguing to take a look at what evidence does exist.

It is generally held that the domestication of wild horses took place in south-west Asia roughly five thousand years before Christ. One of the most popularly held theories about the ancestry of the Camargue horses is rooted in an archaeological discovery which can be dated to at least ten thousand years before domestication can have taken place. In southern Burgundy a limestone cliff rises dramatically above the surrounding vineyards of the Mâconnais like a giant chimney. The cliff is known as the Rock of Solutré; and in the mid-nineteenth century archaeologists excavating the area round the base of the "chimney" came across a vast quantity of animal bones, which lay only a little below the surface and in a layer which extended over almost an acre of land. In places the deposit was as much as six feet in depth. Some of the bones were of reindeer, bison and woolly mammoth, but the great majority were the bones of horses. The site was evidently prehistoric, and the bones were believed—correctly—to date from between 15,000 to 12,000 BC.

Speculation then took over. The favoured view at the time was that the hoard of bones represented some kind of religious rite in which herds of wild horses, as well as other animals, were ceremonially driven along the shallow northern slope of the rock, and so terrorized that they plunged over the sheer cliff to their death. It was never satisfactorily explained how woolly mammoths could be so obligingly terrorized in this fashion. None the less this gruesomely picturesque interpretation remained the accepted view until the 1920s, when a more scientific excavation revealed that none of the bones bore the kind of fractures consistent with horses which had plunged to their death from a great height. As a result the theory of lemming-like suicide became replaced by the more utilitarian view that Stone Age huntsmen had discovered a way of trapping the herds of wild horses against the flank of the cliff as they made their twice-yearly migration north and south, and then killed them for food. That wild horses were regularly hunted in Neolithic times is known from cave paintings not far from Solutré, notably the famous hunting scenes in the Lascaux caves. As for the vast concentration of bones beneath the cliff, one has to assume that the slaughter took place regularly over a period of centuries, if not millennia, and that since Stone Age man had no easy means of transporting dead horses, villagers must have hacked off the meat they wanted on the spot, leaving the carcasses to rot away where they had fallen.

So much for the hunt and the slaughter. No indisputable link exists between the prehistoric horses of Solutré and those of the Camargue today; the span of time is simply too great, and the oceans of space are impossible to bridge. Even so, there are useful pointers. Zoologists have established that there is a strong similarity between the skeletons of the two breeds. Furthermore the Solutré wild horses were certainly migratory and therefore capable of travelling great distances. Southern Burgundy is not an insuperable distance from the Camargue, and the two regions are linked by rivers—the Rhône and its tributary the Saône—along the banks of which migratory herds may easily have travelled north and south according to the seasons. The earliest historical record we have of horses in the region of the Camargue is a Phoenician account from about 2500 BC of herds grazing on pastures lining the lower reaches of the Rhône, and— what is more—being hunted by man for meat. And since they were hunted they must have been wild, not domesticated, even though some breeds of horses had by this time been domesticated for more than two thousand years.

Even though the Camargue horses never seem to have been migratory, Baroncelli believed that here lay evidence enough to establish a link. He was convinced that the breed of wild horse whose remains were found beneath the Solutré cliff were the true ancestors of the present-day Camargue race. It was characteristic of the marquis that this conviction should also become the cornerstone of a far broader set of beliefs concerning the primeval relationship between man and horses. For Baroncelli horsemen were, as he put it, "the first occupants of the soil". There was, he believed, a symbiotic relationship between man and horse, and this bond represented in his mind the very core of human civilization. It was a belief, an act of faith, which goes a long way to explaining the marquis' lifelong commitment to the Camargue as a place to live and work, and in particular to the role of the *manadier*. This commitment was not to a mere country pursuit, a rural game, an escapist's self-indulgence, but was the very essence of life as he saw it. And in order to understand Baroncelli, and some of the far-fetched notions which he held dear (see the following chapter) it is necessary to grasp this unswerving act of faith.

There are a number of alternative views on the ancestry of the Camargue horses. In popular mythology they are said to have originated from horses which once drew the chariot of Poseidon across the oceans, the whiteness of their coats being the foam from the sea. This uniform whiteness, which is a feature of the entire breed, is what makes the Camargue horses unusual. (The foals are actually born brown, and their coats only begin to turn white or, more accurately, greyish-white, after their fourth winter.) Surprisingly—and here is another unexpected link with prehistory—the only early record of another breed of horse having this particular pigmentation is a report by the Greek historian Herodotus in the fifth century BC, in which he writes of "the all-white horses" living in the Pripet marshes of Central Europe. Perhaps it is no coincidence that these horses, like those in the Camargue, also flourished in wetlands.

This record by Herodotus has provided support for another strongly held view of the origin of the Camargue horses, which is that their ancestors came originally from Central Asia, and were brought westwards into Europe as semi-domesticated animals during the early migration of Tartars from Siberia. And if Siberia is to be considered the original homeland of the Camargue horses, then there could be a link, even if a tenuous one, to the celebrated Przewalski horses of Mongolia, the only surviving breed of wild horse in the world today—though this argument becomes a jigsaw puzzle in which far too many pieces are missing.

One further theory, strongly supported by experts, is that the Camargue race derives from horses native to North Africa, where they became domesticated by the Berbers and were subsequently brought across to Europe by Saracen invaders when they occupied most of Spain in the eighth century, and then made repeated forays north of the Pyrenees and along the Mediterranean coast including Languedoc and Provence—and therefore, of course, the Camargue. But then this argument, too, seems undermined by evidence that horses actually existed in the Camargue during Roman times many centuries before the Saracen invasions, and indeed long before Islam existed. Julius Caesar is said to have greatly admired the strength and stamina of the local breed of horse, and to have established farms where they could breed in the region—perhaps associ-

Prehistoric wall-paintings of bulls, deer and horses in the Lascaux caves.

ated with those six thousand veterans of the 6th Roman Legion whom he settled here. In other words the Camargue may have been the stud farm of the Roman *Provincia* as well as its granary.

There can be no clear-cut answer. Theories will roll on and on. That a veil of mystery should hang over the ancestry of the Camargue's horses seems appropriate for a creature which still belongs more to the wild than it does to man; and appropriate too for a region where so many myths have bred and flourished. The horses join the gypsies, the saints, the black bulls, the flamingos, the lost crusaders and the lost monks in creating a mystery play out of the story of this wilderness.

At least the subsequent history of the breed is well enough charted. In the sixteenth century the visiting lord mentioned in the previous chapter, Pierre Quiqueran de Beaujeu, wrote in his survey of the region: "If I make myself speak of this horse, the noblest and most generous that the centuries have ever celebrated, I would not be able to stop." He goes on to record that there were no fewer than four thousand brood mares in the delta, though, as with the figure he quoted for the number of bulls, he may have been the victim of optimistic *manadiers* keen to impress their grand visitor. But even allowing for some exaggeration it is evident that the Camargue possessed almost as many horses in the sixteenth century as it does today.

So what were they used for in such large numbers? The answer has to be partly conjectural. We know that in later centuries they were harnessed for threshing grain and for ploughing, as well as for guarding the bulls, and in all likelihood these had long been their primary roles, possibly ever since the days when the Camargue was the granary of Roman Gaul. It was evidently the mares who did the threshing, treading the stacked sheaves while attached by a long rein to a central wheel, called a *rodo*. Characteristically only the pure-bred Camargue horses were considered hardy enough. Research conducted in recent years has shown that a team of mares working for ten hours a day in a threshing mill covered a distance totalling fifty miles. This as it happens was more or less the same distance that Marquis Baroncelli would regularly ride from near Les Saintes-Maries to Avignon. The proverbial stamina of the Camargue horse must have been mental as much as physical.

At the very end of the eighteenth century another fate was imposed on the hapless creatures. Napoleon decided that the Camargue horse, being sturdy and possessing exceptional powers of endurance, would be ideal for his light cavalry. He must already have been familiar with the breed since a stud had been established in the Camargue since 1727 on the orders of Louis XIV specifically to produce horses for the royal stable, probably at Versailles. But the young general wanted them for military purposes, not for display; and furthermore he wanted them in quantity—"the greatest number possible in order to furnish our Great Army," he declared, "removing from the stock the most beautiful ones to be found." It made excellent sense for Napoleon to use a native breed, over which he could exercise powers and which were therefore readily available. From now onwards not only was the stock of Camargue horses continually bled of its finest animals, but they also began to be crossed with the robust, desert-bred race of Arab stallions, mostly from studs in Spain, the purpose being to improve their temperament, their looks and their speed. (Napoleon himself loved to ride Arab horses in battle, his favourite being the legendary Marengo, a hero of many campaigns, finally captured at the battle of Waterloo and brought in triumph by Wellington to England.)

The practice of breeding and cross-breeding Camargue horses for military purposes persisted for more than a century after Napoleon's defeat and exile. The effect on the breed, both in numbers and in terms of its purity, was not far short of disastrous. It has been estimated that by the end of the First World War only a very small number of the pure-bred Camargue horses had survived. Few of the *manadiers* were engaged in maintaining the original strain, and most of the *gardians* now rode different breeds of horse.

Then, mercifully, military technology came to the rescue, in the shape of an invention which finally made horses redundant on the battlefield. And so it was that the survival of the Camargue horse was ensured in the nick of time by the arrival of the iron horse—the tank.

Chapter Nine

FAME AND REDSKINS

In 1953 an award-winning film, which was shown worldwide, boosted public interest in the Camargue to an unprecedented degree. The region was suddenly famous from South Africa to Japan, and it was the beginning of the tourist boom. The title of the film was *Le Crin Blanc*, meaning "white mane", the mane, of course, being that of a Camargue horse. The production was a collaboration between a well-known director and author, Albert Lamorisse, and a prominent local *manadier* and photographer, Denys Colomb de Daunant, who at that time was the owner of a handsome property called the Mas de Cacherel, a short distance from Les Saintes-Maries-de-la-Mer overlooking one of the larger lagoons. The film told a romantic adventure story of a young boy—a true child of nature—and his beloved white stallion which he rides bare-back across the dunes and into the sea pursued by horse-thieves. Although the plot was fictional, Colomb de Daunant, who conceived the idea as well as providing the horses and much else, happened also to have been the grandson-in-law of no less a figure than Marquis Folco de Batoncelli-Javon.

It comes as no surprise, then, that the young hero of the film should be named Folco. In effect *Le Crin Blanc* was an imaginary re-creation of the life and passions of the young Baroncelli, a posthumous tribute to the great man who had died ten years earlier. The film helped to ensure that the fame and aura of the marquis would never be permitted to perish with him. He became—and still remains—the revered father-figure of the Camargue.

Memories of him, along with the many myths which have surrounded him, are kept alive in the Musée Baroncelli set in the heart of Les Saintes-Maries-de-la-Mer. In addition to his library, his own writings and much personal memorabilia, the museum contains displays illustrating the traditional rural life of the Camargue as he knew it and as he lived it. Packed into the narrow space of the museum are further displays relating to the annual gypsy ceremonies in Les Saintes-Maries, to local flora and fauna, and to Van Gogh who spent several days in the town drawing and painting at just about the time that the nineteen-year-old Baroncelli would first have explored the Camargue with the tragic sentiments of Mistral's *Mirèio* pounding in his heart.

Personal recollections of Baroncelli in his vigorous years are now very few indeed. One such memory comes from a distinguished French poet and novelist, Frédéric Jacques Temple, who has lived in this region all his long life. "In my childhood," he writes,

> every year I used to spend the time of the autumn grape-harvest at a property belonging to my family called the Ilot des Bécasses [meaning "Domain of the Woodcocks"] which was on the banks of the Grand Rhône. We only had to cross the river to find ourselves in the Camargue. One day in September 1928 my parents took me to visit Folco de Baroncelli, the "marquis", in his farmhouse the Mas de l'Amarée. I have a vivid recollection of this short stocky man with a moustache who was wearing an old velvet jacket, boots, a felt hat and a small red silk scarf round his neck to protect him from the mosquitoes. It was said that he spent his entire life on horseback, and that he never dismounted even to sleep. The great moment in my

life was when he lifted me up to ride pillion behind him, and together we galloped for several minutes among his bulls. It is a memory which remains as fresh as ever with me eighty years later. I always regret not having been photographed with this "Centaur" for whom the Camargue was his kingdom.

The Camargue was always Baroncelli's destiny. His mentor, Mistral, even willed it to be so: *Je te laisse la Camargue*, he pronounced in the resigned tone of a man who found it hard to comprehend why anyone in his right mind should choose to live in a wilderness. The link with Mistral was more than that between master and pupil: there was a certain parallel between Baroncelli's passion for the Camargue as a place to live and work and Mistral's more intellectual concern to resurrect the language and culture of the region. Baroncelli himself acknowledged this connection. He had always wanted, he explained later in his life, to achieve with his horses and bulls what the poet had achieved with language. Purity of breed was a complement to purity of language.

The word "purity" features prominently in the statements of both men. Whether their theme was bulls or the Provençal language, at the root of both preoccupations lay an insistence on the value of ancestry, on the need to return to origins, in the shared conviction that a pure Provençal fountain had once flowed but had become muddied by alien influences, principally from France. It was a belief which fuelled a yearning by men such as Mistral and Baroncelli to re-create an identity for this whole region by giving it back those essential elements which had been corrupted by the "invader" or, out of inertia, been allowed to wither away. In this sense these dual ambitions were intensely political. In Baroncelli's words, "it seemed to me that the local passion for bulls was the best means of raising up our people and reviving their national consciousness." This was nothing less than a rallying-call. Whether it was through the cultivation of bulls or the cultivation of the Provençal language, here was a quest, a longing, for an idealized and long-lost Occitania, even though as a coherent and unified state, politically and culturally, Occitania had never actually existed. None the less it was a

concept that was felt to be true. And in this spirit of resurgent nationalism the Camargue became one of the most potent symbols of that
longed-for nation.

Amid the insistent trumpeting for a Provençal utopia a more down-
to-earth note could always be heard, and it was one that has found increasingly receptive ears in a world hounded by fears of climate change
and the wilful destruction of our environment. It was a cry for conservation. Baroncelli's motive for living the life of a *manadier* was not
simply a love of bulls, horses and equestrian games; it was also part of
a profound conviction that man's relationship with nature was essential
for his very soul. As Robert Zaretsky has succinctly put it, Baroncelli
held "the realisation that man risked his very humanity by destroying
the natural world."

Much of the Camargue's present mystique derives from this belief,
so passionately cultivated by Baroncelli and those around him, that here
was a crucial testing-ground for man's relationship with nature. Because
it was a place teeming with wildlife but also teeming with tourists, it was
utterly special in that respect. It was a new Garden of Eden in which
man could choose either to flourish or to fall. And indeed, the subsequent fortunes of this region have demonstrated how apt were those
forebodings. How many hotels, bars, yachting marinas, car parks, horse-
riding treks, not to mention low-flying aircraft and industrial pollution, can a Garden of Eden reasonably sustain? And how much should
commercial interests be allowed to rule?

The ghost of the marquis may well be a troubled spirit today.

The search for the Camargue's unique identity persisted more or less
throughout the entire period of fifty years that Baroncelli spent there,
with the marquis himself forever leading the way. It was a search which
in the process led to some curious destinations. In 1904 he set up a
body entitled *Lou Comitat Virginien*, the Committee for the Festival of
the Virgins. The idea was to bring to the heart of the Camargue, to Les

Saintes-Maries-de-la-Mer, the same annual celebration of female beauty as Mistral had successfully inaugurated in Arles' Roman amphitheatre. As in so many areas Baroncelli was keen to transplant Mistral's ideas to a rural setting. It may be that utopian dreamers in general have a tendency to make a cult of women's virginity, and perhaps in Roman Catholic countries this is an offshoot of the cult of the Virgin Mary, though in Baroncelli's case it is more likely to have been another manifestation of his longing for purity. After the pure race of bulls and the pure race of Camargue horses, why not a pure race of beautiful women? And if all this sounds chillingly familiar in the wake of events in Nazi Germany thirty years later, then comparisons should not be drawn too closely. Here in the Camargue the Festival of the Virgins was never associated with any glorification of a master race; it was more a display of sanitized idealism in the spirit of those chocolate-box images of female perfection fashionable at that time among painters in the Paris Salon, and in England in the High Victorian canvases of Lord Leighton and Sir Lawrence Alma-Tadema.

To be fair to those involved in this ludicrous festival, what mattered most about the women taking part in Baroncelli's *Festo Vierginenco* in Les Saintes-Maries was not only that they should be young and beautiful (and presumably virgins), but that they should be wearing costumes that were traditional to the region. Like the attendants in Mistral's Musée Arlaten, it was essential that they should carry the banner, so to speak, of Occitania. Life in the Camargue was becoming something of a costume drama. Baroncelli would certainly have found it hard to recognize a demonstration of the pure rustic life if the female participants were wearing T-shirts and jeans. Occitania required a uniform.

It also required a symbol. The *gardians*, it is true, already carried their flag of St. George spearing the dragon with his Camargue trident and so rescuing the hapless maiden (another virgin). But that was only for the *Nacioun gardiano*. The Camargue as a whole required a symbol that was all-embracing. And thanks once again to the marquis, in 1926 they finally got one. The Camargue Cross is an impressive object; in ignorance one could easily believe its design to have evolved from some arcane manuscript of the early Christian era. In fact at the invitation of Baroncelli it was dreamed up by an artist named Paul Herman and forged by a local blacksmith. It is a complex design: at the base is an anchor, which is inverted to support a heart, from which rises a cross whose upright and two arms are in the form of a *gardian*'s three-pronged trident. The anchor symbolizes hope, the heart charity, and the cross faith—maintained here appropriately by the *gardians*. Eventually the newly-invented cross was mounted handsomely on a limestone base and erected a short distance from Les Saintes-Maries close to where the marquis had by now built himself a house, Mas du Simbeu. The house no longer stands, but the cross remains, a lone sentinel and witness to Baroncelli's hopes and ambitions. And if it bear a strong resemblance to a medieval preaching cross, then what could be more appropriate?

It was inevitable with so many "nationalist" sentiments aroused by these displays of regional pride that passions should be directed against the seat of French authority, Paris. The history of the south ensured that anti-French sentiments were virtually endemic to the entire region, and these sentiments were fanned and fostered by the young intellectuals, writers and journalists who were associated with Mistral and his circle, all of whom were happy to seize any opportunity to foment public resentment of Paris in the name of a downtrodden but now gloriously renascent Occitania.

A prime opportunity for such agitation occurred early in the twentieth century. Mistral was by now a venerable Nobel Prize-winning author and sage loftily holding court in Avignon, while the young Baroncelli was already entrenched in his rustic life of *manadier*-cum-poet in the depths of the Camargue.

The event in question, later to be labelled *La Révolution du Midi*, was the wine-growers' strike of 1907. By this time the southern region of France, Languedoc in particular, had become responsible for producing more than one-third of the nation's wine. But unlike other wine-producing areas of France, the economy of Languedoc had been allowed to become virtually a monoculture; and when a severe economic recession overtook France late in the nineteenth century cheaper imports of wine from Spain and Algeria began to reduce an ever-increasing number of wine-growers of the south to impoverishment. Georges Clemenceau's government did nothing to assist them, and bankrupt farms were seized by officials. Early in 1907 the Languedoc farmers became organized enough to mount angry demonstrations against the Paris authorities. Many thousands of *vignerons* marched through the streets of Narbonne. Soon afterwards an even greater number marched through the nearby town of Béziers. In the spring a demonstration in the austere Protestant city of Montpellier was estimated to have numbered almost half a million. If this may appear excessive given that that it was three times the population of the city, then the very exaggeration may be seen as a measure of the level of public feeling at this time. A month later a similar protest was held in Nîmes, in which it was reported that a local villager strode through the crowd wielding a Camargue *gardian*'s trident to which a banner was attached bearing the legend in Occitan declaring (as translated): "If we cannot sell our wine we will go to work with our iron tridents."

When President Clemenceau finally resorted to sending in the military to occupy the region, the troops, being local recruits, refused to do so, to the further embarrassment of Paris, and it required soldiers hastily drafted in from North Africa to do the job—which they did reluctantly and with little conviction. None the less the "invasion" was sufficient to arouse bitter comparisons with the bloodiest episode in the history of the south, the notorious Albigensian Crusade conducted by French troops from the north who had brutally crushed the heretical Cathars in Languedoc in the thirteenth century. Downtrodden people have long memories, and now it seemed to many in the towns and villages of the south that the same act of barbarism was being re-enacted before their eyes. Tempers were at boiling-point at every level of society, and Languedoc probably never came closer to devolution from France than at this moment. Marquis Baroncelli was among those whose rage could no longer be contained. The *gardians*' trident, from being a peaceful instrument for guiding the Camargue bulls, was suddenly a symbol of political resistance. And in the tradition of the Félibrige poets, of which Baroncelli had been one, the marquis let fly in verse. His poem, published widely, was called *Auzor* ("Arise"), and it was a clarion call. "Poor people of the Midi," it began, "six hundred years of emasculation and slaughter have marked you so deep that your face is wreathed in sorrow." He then warmed to his theme: "Pale-faced northerners who rejoice over our difficulties: we shall gut your entrails the day all hell breaks loose."

Only someone fluent in Occitan would be qualified to pronounce on whether these sentiments have a more poetic ring in the vernacular. Mistral, still loftily holding court in Avignon, certainly did not think so. In the manner of a tutor remonstrating with a pupil for writing an abysmal essay he denounced the poem as a crude explosion of bombast. Baroncelli did his best to shrug off the reprimand from the master; none the less the poem, as well as the whole episode of the wine-growers' protest, cast the seemingly gentle marquis in the role of a sabre-rattling patriot in the cause of his beloved south. He even made a virtue of the discomforts of the Camargue itself. "Let us bless the mosquitoes, gnats and midges," he pronounced: "They guard us as best they can from the Foreigner!" From being a new Garden of Eden the Camargue was beginning to sound like a battlefield.

The *Révolution du Midi* eventually petered out with the gradual improvement of the economic climate, but more particularly in the face of a greater national crisis, the outbreak of the First World War. The Camargue may have been about as far from the war zone as it was possible to be in France; none the less Languedoc and the south in general suffered just as severely as other regions in the calamitous loss of manpower between 1914 and 1918, as local war memorials testify. To this day there are villages whose resident population is fewer than the number of men from the community killed in the First World War.

There were two deaths that took place during those years which had a special poignancy for the region, and for Marquis Baroncelli in particular. On the eve of the outbreak of war Frédéric Mistral died in his beloved village of Maillane. Relations between the two men had been little more than respectful for many years, and had grown distinctly cooler following Baroncelli's crude outburst in verse over the wine-growers' protest, which the Nobel Prize winner clearly felt to be unworthy of the Provençal literary renaissance he had so long championed. Besides, Mistral had never really understood why a man as talented and privileged as the marquis should have chosen to abandon the civilized world of letters for a rustic existence among the bulls and the mosquitoes.

Baroncelli for his part, and in spite of disagreements with Mistral, had never entirely shed the role of acolyte. Moreover, this role of respectful follower was never more evident than in his connection with the second figure whose death occurred during those war years. That man was Colonel William Cody, otherwise known as Buffalo Bill.

The relation between Baroncelli and Buffalo Bill's Wild West Show led to one of the most surreal episodes in the story of the Camargue. The background, in brief, is this. William Cody had served in the American Civil War, and subsequently worked for the US Army as a civilian scout, distinguishing himself as a marksman and buffalo-hunter. He went on to work as a guide for the US Cavalry in the government's campaign to crush Indian resistance against ejection from their tradi-

From a photograph of Baroncelli with one of his daughters.

tional territories west of the Mississippi. The most notorious incident in that rebellion was the defeat and scalping of General Custer's band of soldiers at Little Big Horn River by a party of Indians led by the chief of the Dakota Sioux, Sitting Bull. Cody's equally notorious response had been to hunt down and scalp an Indian chief in repayment for the massacre at Little Big Horn, after which he was awarded a Medal of Honour. To Cody's buccaneer image was added a growing reputation for being—ironically—an expert on all matters relating to Indian life and culture. It was this combined gift of showmanship and knowledge of Indian affairs which led to the setting up of Cody's theatrical extravaganza known as the Wild West Show, in which he took the name Buffalo Bill (appropriately since he had once slaughtered more than 4,000 of them). Thereafter, from 1889 Cody regularly toured Europe with his troupe of Indians to a tumultuous reception from all who flocked to see them—including Queen Victoria, who sat through the four-hour performance three times.

Buffalo Bill's connection with Languedoc came about originally through Frédéric Mistral (see Chapter 3), though it is unclear precisely how it took place. We know that several of Cody's Indian performers were in the Camargue at the end of the year 1905. Since this was only one year after Mistral had achieved international celebrity by being awarded the Nobel Prize, it is more than likely that Cody chose this moment to accept an invitation from the famous author to extend his tour of Europe by coming south. Here, as Mistral would have assured him, his cowboys would find much in common with the local *gardians*. One of the many bizarre aspects of Cody's bandwagon as it trundled round the country was his fondness of posing for photographs next to the principal Indian in his show. Both men were photographed dressed in their full regalia—the Indian as a Sioux warrior swathed in eagles' feathers, Cody himself as a marksman and intrepid hunter—but with no hint of an acknowledgment that both men had in their time been identified with a conflict involving the scalping of warriors on either side.

It was on 7 December of that year, 1905, as described by Robert

Zaretsky, that a gathering of *gardians* took place near the village of Le Cailar, on the edge of the Camargue, in order to select bulls for an *abrivado*. Among those present at this seemingly minor affair were not only Marquis Folco de Baroncelli-Javon but also two Dakota Sioux chiefs, Iron Tail and Lone Bull.

What followed was reportedly a breakfast shared by Baroncelli, several other friends as well as the distinguished Indian visitors, at which champagne was opened and a toast raised to "the health of those races who refused to surrender", after which the party "conversed about Mistral, the Félibrige, and Provence." This was followed by a motor cavalcade in which the Indians stood up and delivered their famous war-chant.

This brief (and extraordinarily unlikely) account of events at Le Cailar was duly published in a Provençal language newspaper under a pseudonym which concealed the fact that the author was none other than Baroncelli himself. Whatever the truthfulness or otherwise of the report it was the beginning of an often tortuous saga involving the marquis and his impassioned involvement with American West. Whereas Mistral's relationship with the Wild West Show was with its founder, Buffalo Bill—a cordial meeting of two celebrities—Baroncelli was drawn to the Indians themselves. From now onwards the marquis was to become obsessed with what he perceived to be the parallel plight and destiny of the American Redskins and the downtrodden people of Occitania. As Zaretsky puts it, "The Camargue became 'le Far-West'."

Early the following year Baroncelli travelled to Paris especially in order to meet Buffalo Bill and to renew his acquaintance with his Indians. Here he met a young Sioux chief, Jacob White Eyes, with whom he formed a friendship which was among the closest of his life. It was accompanied by a lengthy correspondence which regularly crisscrossed the Atlantic for many years long after White Eyes had returned to his native Dakota. The marquis was even happy to be awarded an honorary Indian name, Zind-Kala-Waste, meaning Faithful One; and there is a surviving photograph (in the Baroncelli Museum in Les Saintes-Maries-de-la-Mer) of a smiling marquis enveloped in an Indian feathered headdress, though with no accompanying tomahawk.

Shortly after that first meeting in Paris the Wild West Show took off again for Languedoc. Before it left the capital Baroncelli wrote to Jacob White Eyes, "I have the impression that I was an Indian in a previous life. When I see you, I feel that I am once again with long-lost brothers." When the show arrived in the south later that year, the marquis faithfully followed it from location to location: Toulouse, Avignon, Nîmes and finally home territory, Les Saintes-Maries. Here the Indians pitched their wigwams in the grounds of his farmhouse, the Mas de l'Amarée, and joined in the equestrian displays that formed part of Baroncelli's *Festo Vierginenco*, the annual Festival of the Virgins which he had recently inaugurated. And so the Camargue enjoyed its first taste of the Wild West, complete with tomahawks, feathered headdresses and spine-chilling war-cries. The marquis was in his dreamland.

He was certainly not alone in holding this mythical view of the American West: it was one that had been richly fed by fashionable literature of the time. One of the most internationally popular novelists when Baroncelli was a young man was the American James Fenimore Cooper, whose *The Last of the Mohicans* (1826) contributed greatly to a cult of the Wild West in Europe and beyond. Cowboys and Indians caught the imagination of the reading public worldwide. In France a romantic novelist of the same era was Gustave Aimard, whose prolific output included such pulse-raising titles as *Les Trappeurs de l'Arkansas* and *Les Bandites de l'Arizona*. Baroncelli owned quantities of Aimard's books.

Few readers of adventure novels, however wild their imagination might be, had ever been anywhere near the American West. In the pre-cinema age the popular image of Red Indians and their life and culture was derived almost exclusively from romantic fiction, until suddenly—with the arrival of Buffalo Bill and his troupe—the image was accessible at first hand. The charge that the Wild West Show was only an entertainment, like the circus, could easily be dismissed because here, after all, were genuine Indian chiefs with genuine wigwams, tomahawks and war-dances, and bearing authentic-sounding names like Iron Tail and White Eyes. What was more, the American Indians fitted perfectly into a mythical type with which Frenchmen were already familiar. Anyone brought up on the writings of Jean-Jacques Rousseau and Chateaubriand was thoroughly at home with the romantic concept of the "noble savage", that heroic soul who belonged to a race of people whose isolation had spared them the corrupting influence of "civilization".

Now, instead of being a mere idea dreamed up by philosophers, here the "noble savage" was—in the heart of Europe, tomahawk and all.

Baroncelli's obsession with the American Indians can sound naïve and sentimental, but it can also be seen to explain, more than anything else we know about the marquis, what drove the man to lead the life he led, and where his deepest convictions lay. This aristocratic figure, titled, well-educated and well-connected, none the less felt himself to be a member of a misunderstood and disadvantaged people, and passionately seized the chance to identify himself with a people that he considered to be similarly downtrodden. They were also both of them people who lived their days on horseback. To compare the condition of the Provençals with that of the American Indians may sound far-fetched in the extreme; even so he considered it to be valid, and it became his crusading banner, his war-cry. It was a crusade that led Baroncelli to embrace a number of tenets of faith in which factual evidence played only the smallest part, if any part at all. He believed he had himself been a Red Indian in a previous life. He held the view that the gypsies who paid their annual pilgrimage to the Camargue were in origin part of the same nomadic people as the American Indians, and that they were actually descendants of the inhabitants of Atlantis, who had become divided from their American cousins by a giant earthquake in the Atlantic during the Bronze Age. The gypsies, furthermore, came to the Camargue to worship at the shrine of Sara because, he claimed, she was a priestess of the cult of Mithras, which in turn linked them with the Provencal cult of the bull—to which he had devoted his own life.

So, somehow in his mind it all fitted together.

It was a beguiling mix of convictions, even if—not surprisingly—there were those around the marquis who politely considered his views to belong more to cloud-cuckoo-land than to the Rhône delta.

The suggestion that Baroncelli somehow "invented" the culture of the Camargue rests on the claim that he created a fictitious history and mythology in order to justify the sporting activities he promoted—the bull games and equestrian events. What is certainly true is that in a spirit of passionate conviction he endowed the region with a wealth of unorthodox opinions which succeeded in giving the Camargue a colourful and exotic flavour (witness his views on a Mithraic bull cult dating back to pre-Roman times, on his own reincarnation as a born-again Red Indian, on Atlantis, on the supposed ethnic links between gypsies and Redskins, and so on).

Yet at the same time none of these personally-held convictions made any actual impact on the culture and character of the Camargue as we know it. The bulls and horses which roam the delta were here long before Baroncelli. So were the flamingos, the *gardians* and the salt mountains. So were the gypsies and the cult of black Sara. So too were the Three Marys, the great fortified church and the annual pilgrimage to the sea. And so (as we know from Van Gogh's letter to his brother Theo) were the bull games, the *course libre*, as well as the Spanish-style bullfights in the Roman arenas. In fact Baroncelli's sole original contribution seems to have been the *Festo Vierginenco*, which mercifully died an early death, so saving any number of maiden blushes.

Baroncelli's most vivid contribution to the culture of the Camargue was simply to dress it up. He gave the region a striking emblem in the form of a symbolic cross. He gave the *gardians* a recognizable costume. He did the same for the *razeteurs* in the bull games, making sure that they no longer looked like second-class Spanish toreadors. And like Mistral before him he championed the local Arlesian costumes and the traditional motifs which they bore—today an attractive feature of shirts, waistcoats and skirts sold to tourists in the local markets.

He was never, in other words, the inventor of the Camargue; he was its choreographer and ringmaster. If he was an inventor at all, then he was the inventor of himself. He was a man who wove his own personal mythology and spread it lightly around him and across the landscape he loved.

Most of all, his contribution was to the Camargue as a place. Baroncelli was among the first to champion the view that certain landscapes are as worthy of preservation as any palace or cathedral. He was one of the great pioneers of the conservation movement. And for this, if for no other reason, he deserves his seat of honour in the watery pantheon of the Camargue.

Late in his life the marquis built himself a house on a piece of land which he owned near the mouth of the Petit Rhône a short distance to the west of Les Saintes-Maries-de-la-Mer. For many decades previously he had lived in a farmhouse he had rented, the Mas de l'Amarée. Now he was close to the sea, close to the river, and within sight of the pilgrimage church where the gypsies congregated and where in his view the cult of Mithras and its associated bull-worship had been practised. Appropriately he named the new house after a famous bull, Simbeu, a word that also meant "symbol", which seems equally appropriate.

For a while an autumnal glow lit up the marquis' life. Although the Second World War had broken out, Provence and Languedoc were part of unoccupied Vichy France. In April 1941 a theatrical performance was held in Arles' Roman amphitheatre in honour of the 81-year-old Baroncelli. The occasion was attended by the wife of Marshal Pétain, head of the Vichy government and the hero of Verdun, at which the hero of the Camargue was thanked on behalf of the French nation for having saved "the soul of the land".

The glow did not last long. With the threat of Allied landings in the Mediterranean the Vichy government collapsed and the German armies marched into the south. In November 1942 German troops occupied the Mas du Simbeu. In February the following year Baroncelli found himself evicted from the house he had built for himself, and he was compelled to return to Avignon, by now depressed and sick. The Germans proceeded to destroy the house to make way for blockhouses against any forthcoming landings by Allied troops (though before long they retreated north without a shot being fired). By now seriously ill, the marquis none the less made a farewell ride back to Les Saintes-Maries-de-la-Mer accompanied by one of his faithful *gardians*. Then, ten days before Christmas, not long after riding back to Avignon, Baroncelli died. He was 83. The funeral took place in the lovely Gothic church of St.-Agricol, in the heart of the city close to the former family Palais du Roure.

This was not quite the end of the story. It seems appropriate for a man around whom so many myths had gathered that there should have been one final Camargue performance, one which the marquis' ghost might well have choreographed. Almost eight years after his death Baroncelli's ashes were ceremonially returned home. The little train which then operated from Arles brought his remains back to Les Saintes-Maries where a funeral cortege was waiting. After a service in the church the casket was lifted on the backs of twelve gypsies who bore it out of the town to where the marquis' house had once stood. A herd of black bulls is said to have followed the funeral procession, while flamingos formed a scarlet fly-past over the nearby lagoon. And here on the site of his former *mas* he was buried. Since it was a casket of ashes rather than a coffin the occasion was not exactly as he had once requested, but it was true in spirit to his final wish: "Take my body and bury me at the earth at Simbeu, my head facing the house I lived in and my feet turned towards the church of Saintes-Maries: that is where I want to sleep."

Chapter Ten

BALANCING ACTS

The topography of the Camargue, and how it is divided up and variously owned, can look like a jigsaw puzzle of which several key pieces always seem to be missing, or else the picture has become indistinct—"washed away" might be a more appropriate term. In theory it ought to be simple. In 1970 the entire area became a French Regional National Park, one of forty-five in the country to date, the aim of which was to ensure that the private and public interests vested in the delta could be sensibly balanced: rice-growing, stock-breeding, sheep-grazing, duck-shooting, building-works in general, wildlife of all kinds, and of course the commercial interest which was already expanding faster than all the rest—tourism.

Whatever the passionate concerns of bird-watchers and nature-lovers may be, the crude fact is that the major income of the Camargue derives from the tourist trade. The region attracts more than one million visitors each year, mostly in the summer months, and mostly in search of some of the finest beaches in the Mediterranean. Much of the entire length of Camargue coastline is that rarity in twenty-first-century Europe, an unbroken stretch of sand uncluttered by hotels, apartment blocks, kebab stalls, shopping arcades, funfairs, even car-parks—since much of it is accessible only on foot: hence its appeal to lovers of peace, if not always of solitude. A concerted effort to reduce mosquitoes by insecticide spraying in the 1960s and the construction of purpose-built resorts such as the modernist La Grande Motte marked an attempt by politicians and developers to exploit the potential of a hitherto deserted stretch of the Mediterranean, but pockets of wilderness remain.

The most popular and accessible beaches lie on the extreme east and west of the Camargue. Close to the attractive fishing town of Le Grau-du-Roi, a short distance from Aigues-Mortes, is the flourishing resort of Port-Camargue, created from nothing in 1969 and now host to enough yachts to assemble an armada. Along the coast from Port-Camargue runs a stretch of more than ten miles of what a local brochure describes as "golden sand bordered gently by the warm Mediterranean sea" ("gentle", that is to say, when the mistral is not blowing). This is the Plage de l'Espiguette, towards the far end of which stands one of the Camargue's lonelier lighthouses, casting its bleak gaze over a spread of naked marshland on one side and a spread of naked flesh from a nudist colony on the other. Clothed or unclothed, this is a place where the visitor may discover heavenly tranquillity.

Near the eastern extremity of the Camargue is another broad and unspoilt expanse of beach, several miles in length. This is the Plage de Piémanson, also known as the Plage d'Arles, being the closest stretch of sea-coast for visitors driving from the big town past Van Gogh's rebuilt bridge and along the Grand Rhône to the little car ferry close to Port St.-Louis (named after the French king who launched the seventh crusade, not actually from here but from Aigues-Mortes further west). Again, here are no hotels or restaurants; merely the sun and the sea, and a hundred thousand wild birds all around.

For those weary of such things the Camargue has a rich variety other delights to offer the visitor, above all, horse-trekking. More than thirty-five local farms (*manades*) offer horses for hire, or a wide selection of expeditions led by local *gardians* across the marshlands and the shallow lagoons. In addition there are numerous walking trails, and for the less energetic horse-drawn carriages even jet-skis and quad bikes, as well as adventure forests for children and the young at heart.

Needless to say, a combination of quite so many diverse and competing interests was never likely to produce a result to everyone's taste. And so it has proved. The Park has been a battleground as often as a place of peace. Too many of those pieces of jigsaw were never made to fit together. For example, the largest lagoon in the Camargue, the Etang de Vaccarès, which is the heart of one of the most important nature reserves in Europe, depends for its required balance of salt-water and fresh water on a supply from the rice fields to the north and the salt-pans (or the sea) to the south, both supplies being controlled by private commercial interests located beyond the boundaries of the reserve itself.

If this seems like one prescription for disaster, then consider the further fact that the reserve's most glamorous inhabitant, the scarlet flamingo, has traditionally chosen to breed in an area outside the Camargue reserve, in the middle of a lagoon owned by the nearby salt company on whose shoulders rested the sole responsibility for maintaining the level of salt-water necessary if the birds are to breed.

As it transpired, here was not merely a prescription for disaster: it was a disaster which actually struck. In 2007 the salt company, the Salins du Midi, lost its main contract, apparently to Eastern European rivals whose production costs were cheaper. As a result salt production in the eastern Camargue, centring on the small town of Salin-de-Giraud, came to a standstill. In response large numbers of employees of the company came out on strike, fearful for their jobs, salt production being virtually the only source of employment in the town (see Chapter 5). But not only was the production of salt halted: so was the pumping of salt-water into the nearby lagoon where the flamingos annually lay their eggs. This was the small Etang du Fangassier, which lies equidistant between the Vaccarès and the salt-pans, close to one of the "lost" arms of the Rhône still marked on maps as the Vieux Rhône. Flamingos (as will be described in the next chapter) insist on nesting on mud-hillocks that are safely raised above the dangers of flooding but are close enough to shallow water for food to be readily available by means of their elongated legs and scoop-like beaks.

In other words, the requirements of a flamingo breeding colony are precise and uncompromising. Too much water, or too little, and the birds refuse to breed. And in the spring of 2007, because the salt company failed to pump in the salt-water, this is precisely what happened. There were no breeding flamingos in the Camargue for the first time for nearly forty years.

One of the happier by-products of tourism is that the scarlet flamingo is now a star. It pulls in the crowds, and many commercial interests rest on its well-being. Whereas half a century ago a few birdwatchers and dedicated ecologists would have shed tears, and the sad news have made several column-inches in the local Arles newspaper, now in 2007 the non-breeding of the Camargue's star performers hit the world's press and became an acute embarrassment to the French government, as well as being seen as a dark warning that the health of one of Europe's principal nature reserves was desperately fragile. Urgent negotiations took place between the salt company and the government, represented by the Conservatoire du Littoral, a body empowered to safeguarding such areas of the French Mediterranean coastline as have managed to escape the tourist leviathan. As a result of these negotiations, on 29 August 2007 it was announced that the flamingos' nesting-ground, the Etang du Fangassier, was to be one of eleven different sites sold to the French government, amounting to almost six thousand acres in all—or, as the sport-loving local press chose to put it, the equivalent of three thousand rugby pitches.

What this change of ownership meant was that the nesting-site where the flamingos used to breed would now be administered and controlled by wildlife experts, not by a body whose primary interests are commercial, however benevolent they may have been in past years. The new controlling body was to be the Société Nationale de Protection de la Nature, which already administers the Réserve Nationale de Camargue. This effectively meant that the boundary of the present reserve would now stretch further south beyond the Vaccatrès to embrace those smaller lagoons which abut the nineteenth-century seawall, the Digue à la Mer, including of course the all-important Etang du Fangassier. When the announcement of the purchase was made by the French Ecology Minister it was described as an "historic operation". There were many present who felt that the judgment of history would depend on many more issues than the survival of a flamingo breeding colony. The director of the Réserve Nationale, Eric Coulet, wisely placed the new agreement in a wider context: "It is a balance between the river and the sea, between fresh water and salt water, between nature and human activity." And he went on to dwell on the many accompanying threats which hang over the Camargue, among them air pollution and pesticides, as well as the unhealthy condition of the River Rhône itself which, if expert opinion is to be believed, may take up to twenty years to put right. Added to these dire warnings is the proposal, yet to be implemented, to bridge the Grand Rhône close to its mouth near Port St.-Louis. At present there is only a ferry, the nearest bridge across the river being a considerable distance to the north, at Arles. A bridge here, close to St.-Louis, would provide direct motor access to the Camargue from Marseille as well as from the industrial and heavily populated areas immediately to the east of the river—with the inevitable consequence of the whole south-eastern area of the delta being transformed into yet another holiday conurbation with enviably long beaches close at hand.

These are some of the nightmares that haunt the sleep of those for whom the Camargue, however fragile, remains a precious mirror of paradise.

To widespread relief the Camargue woke from its worst nightmare in the summer of 2008. The new controlling body administering the Etang du Fangassier ensured that the required water level at the flamingos' nesting-site was restored. And the birds duly obliged. A spokesman for the Tour du Valat Biological Research Station in the heart of the Camargue confirmed that 10,000 pairs had successfully bred that year.

The situation had returned to normal. Naturalists, tourists and hoteliers alike all breathed a deep sigh of relief. One crisis at least was over—for the time being.

⸎

The Regional National Park of the Camargue comprises more than two hundred thousand acres. This is made up of grazing land, rice fields, woodland, fresh-water channels and lakes, salt-marsh and salt-water lagoons, small towns and villages, innumerable farms and smallholdings of different kinds, as well as an ever-expanding outcrop of hotels and other tourist amenities including yachting harbours and arenas for equestrian events. A recent survey revealed that the region sustained approximately three thousand horses, fifteen thousand bulls of the Camargue variety (those with horns directed upwards) and a further six thousand Spanish-type bulls (with horns directed forwards).

The Park has its own showcase, the Museum of the Camargue, situated in the Mas du Pont du Rousty, a former sheepfold eight miles south-west of Arles (described in Chapters 1 and 5). In addition, scattered across the delta, are numerous nature reserves, most of them with their own information centre offering publications in several languages, videos, CDs and DVDs, as well as bird-watching equipment and brochures proposing guided tours and wildlife walks for the energetic and the less energetic. There are also any number of guided horse-trekking expeditions along the dykes and across the dried salt-marshes, and—for the least energetic of all—"Jeep safaris" in selected areas where wildlife is unlikely to be disturbed.

The foremost among these nature reserves is the one embracing the Camargue's "inland sea", the Etang de Vaccarès. The Réserve Nationale de Camargue touches dry land scarcely at all, though near the eastern shore of the Vaccarès it embraces just enough *terra firma* to house its administrative offices and tourist information centre in a modest-looking former *mas* and hunting-lodge known as La Capelière. This is as good a starting-point as any for a visitor to the Camargue.

Apart from a wealth of literature, a film-show and a permanent exhibition on the area, it proposes a mile-long circuit of a nearby marsh and lagoon described intriguingly as *Le Sentier des Rainettes*, the Footpath of the Tree Frogs. For those starved of exercise after a mere mile the Réserve also offers a three-mile trek a short distance to the south of La Capelière taking in an area of marshland and a salt-lake, the Salin de Badon, which is particularly rich in wildlife and local flora. And for those with an ear for vanished history the longest arm of this walk, *Le Sentier des Foulques* (Footpath of the Falcons), passes close to the site of one of the Camargue's earliest religious settlements, the Cistercian abbey of Ulmet, which was among the number of Camargue "salt monasteries" before it was swept away in the twelfth century by the anger of the Rhône.

From the Salin de Badon the old course of the river is now static, yet on the map it still appears to makes its snake-like journey southwards towards the sea. Shortly before merging into the open lagoons and salt-flats near the coast it describes a final loop past the ruins of one of the many Camargue towers, the Tour de Tourville, constructed during the seventeenth century along the river-banks chiefly to protect Arles from pirates, in particular the marauding Turks and Arab corsairs who were still making the Mediterranean a perilous sea on which to sail.

The road, meanwhile, has veered south-east across the marshlands, bypassing the salt-town of Salin-de-Giraud to follow the last five miles of the Grand Rhône towards one of the most valuable—and certainly the most remote—of the Camargue nature reserves, the Domaine de la Palissade.

This was a privately-owned hunting estate until the whole area, comprising nearly two thousand acres, was bought in 1977 by the Conservatoire du Littoral, the same public body which thirty years later arranged to purchase the flamingos' endangered nesting-ground, the Etang du Fangassier. The special quality of La Palissade is that it is a microcosm of what the entire Camargue used to be up until the mid-nineteenth century when the sea-dyke was constructed and the two branches of the River Rhône were embanked. Situated at the southernmost tip of

the Camargue, it lies beyond both the sea-dyke and the raised banks of
the Grand Rhône; hence it is alarmingly vulnerable to the violence of the
elements—the river and the sea—in a way that no other area of the delta
is affected. The result is some of the wildest and bleakest terrain in the
entire Camargue, though should there ever be a bridge across the Grand
Rhône a short distance upstream, then the fifteen-mile stretch of near-
deserted beach beyond the reserve could turn into yet another summer
playground, and La Palissade become a threatened oasis of raw nature
amid a desert of kebab-stalls and petrol stations.

At present isolation still endows the area with an air of lonely peace.
One of the most remote walks in France, up to four hours of it, can
take you round the perimeter of the central lagoon, the Etang de
Grande Palun, from where you are made soberly aware that nothing
but an uninviting sea lies between here and Africa.

The lagoon itself, being nature's unadulterated cocktail of river-
and sea-water, is home to a particularly rich variety of fish and other sea-
creatures, and in consequence home to an equally large number of
herons and white egrets which feast on them, all of which combines to
make La Palissade one of the most rewarding venues for naturalists in
the whole of the Camargue. On the north side of the reserve stands the
former hunting-lodge, a handsome building which is now an information centre and Maison de la Nature: here the special nature of the flora
and fauna of this micro-region is demonstrated in a rich variety of displays, literature and audiovisual presentations.

The Etang de Vaccarès divides the Lower Camargue into two
"legs", east and west, both with their feet in the Mediterranean. Apart
from the long lonely sea-dyke along which the intrepid may choose to
walk some fifteen miles from one "leg" to the other, the only way from
east to west is by means of the inland road which skirts the northern
shore of the Vaccarès and eventually joins the main highway between
Arles to Les Saintes-Maries-de-la-Mer. Both La Capelière and La
Palissade nature reserves are located in the eastern area of the Camargue.
Several other reserves are located on the western side, in particular the
Ginès Centre, which serves as the information office for the whole

Camargue Regional Park, and its accompanying Bird Park, both of them located just a few miles north of Les Saintes-Maries at Pont de Gau close to a rash of modern hotels determined to look authentic. The Pont de Gau Bird Park is a masterpiece of wilderness-made-easy. It is part-zoo, part-swamp. The main area of the park is the Etang de Ginès, a twenty-acre expanse of lagoon and marsh which is contained enough for a wealth of bird-life to be accessible either from the main road running north towards Arles (the D 570), or from the more attractive minor road to the east of the lagoon (the D 85A) in the direction of Pioch-Badet.

Here, at least for the ornithologist, is the quintessential Camargue. It is all here, and relatively close at hand. Raised pathways wind through the marshes on either side of the central lagoon; and if a visitor's ambition is to watch white egrets and grey or purple herons stalking the shallows, or marsh harriers quartering the reed-beds, and of course scarlet flamingos—then this is the place to be. And for visitors more accustomed to room service there are aviaries covering an area of two acres in which many of the more reclusive local birds are on display in settings that do their best to mimic the wild.

Two further reserves in this western area have a rich appeal to the nature lover, though perhaps to two different kinds of naturalist. To the east of the Etang de Ginès the minor road running north from Les Saintes-Maries skirts a larger lagoon dotted with tiny islands and opening out eastwards on to the vast Vaccarès, and therefore seemingly for ever. Here, on a soft evening, when the lagoon catches fire with the setting sun and the horizon is flagged by a thousand scarlet flamingos, it can be one of the magic moments of the Camargue, and you can understand more than ever why there are people who would move mountains to preserve this place. The inner lagoon bears the official title of Réserve Départementale des Impériaux, and it exists for no more high-flown a reason than to protect the fishing-rights of the local community, the twelve square miles of Les Impériaux having been purchased from the department for this purpose and supervised by the commune of Les Saintes-Maries-de-la-Mer.

The final reserve in this area north of Les Saintes-Maries is La Sigoulette, and here one is expected to do a great deal more than stand around admiring flamingos through binoculars. La Sigoulette is a residential "House of Nature" and a zealously proselytizing organization aimed primarily at the young, the purpose of staying here being to spend each day exploring and studying the reserve's seven hundred acres of typical Camargue terrain under the guidance of teachers and experts. This is a wild-life adventure playground as well as the nearest there is to a boarding-school of the Camargue.

But if there is a nature reserve *de luxe*, then it is one that lies strictly speaking outside the Camargue. This is a 2,500-acre expanse of marshland and lagoons called the Marais du Vigueirat, and it forms the northern section of the region immediately to the east of the Grand Rhône known as Le Grand Plan du Bourg. Geographically it is identical to the Camargue, and was created by the same conditions of floodwater spilling out from the Rhône and from the sea over a period of so many millennia. At the Vigueirat the accustomed attractions of the Camargue

are present in quantity—colourful wading-birds, black bulls, white horses, three miles of raised walkways through the marshes and round the lagoons, even the prospect of wild boar swimming at alarming speed as they head for the woods across the water. In addition, for the benefit of the armchair birdwatcher there is a special facility in the shape of a horse-drawn open carriage designed to take the pain out of walking.

Weather-beaten ornithologists hardened to sun and storms may wince at such pampering, yet it is tourist-focused centres like the Vigueirat, as much as the more hallowed regions of the Camargue, where that most delicate of balancing acts will ultimately be put to the test—the balance between the interests of the natural world and of human beings who share that world, often invasively and in ever-increasing numbers.

In fact the Marais du Vigueirat is a prime testing-ground for this precious balance of interests, since both sides are equally represented here. While all possible facilities are provided for the public to enjoy the reserve's abundance of wildlife, the management and administration of the Vigueirat are in the hands of a private foundation dedicated to conservation and to the promotion of scientific research. The foundation is the offspring of an institution based in a former *domaine* across the river from the Vigueirat, deep in the wooded marshlands of the delta itself, known as La Tour du Valat.

And if the Camargue may be said of possess an engine-room, then it is here.

The story of the Tour du Valat is a stirring one, as well as a testament to one man's personal dedication. He is Dr. Luc Hoffmann, one of the more quietly-sung heroes of the modern Camargue. As a member of the family owning the Swiss pharmaceutical company of Hoffmann-La Roche, the privilege of wealth was always his, and few people have used that privilege to more imaginative effect. Hoffmann first visited the Camargue as a student shortly after the Second World War. Then in 1950, having graduated in biology, he returned and succeeded in buying a four-thousand-acre estate lying between the Vaccarès and the Grand Rhône. The estate was composed of woodland, agricultural land, a freshwater lagoon and marsh (the Marais de St.-Seren), as well as areas of salt-marsh. The name Tour du Valat derives from one of the ancient towers which once guarded a former branch of the Rhône, the same branch that destroyed the abbey of Ulmet a short distance to the south, and still clearly visible on maps in the shape of surviving waterways within the Valat estate.

Hoffmann proceeded to convert the *domaine* into the headquarters of what soon became the Station Biologique de la Tour du Valat. The foundation he established in order to finance its activities had as its aim to "conduct and promote scientific research with special reference to conservation and management of wetland communities in the Camargue." The wording was significant: the concern of the foundation was not only wildlife, but the wellbeing of the entire area, including its rice-growers, stock-breeders, sheep farmers, fishermen, hunters, even tourists. Here was scientific research in the service of a community in all its diversity. It was a pioneering endeavour, and out of it much of what we take for granted as the "modern Camargue" was born.

It is easy to appreciate how insecure the welfare of the Camargue must have appeared at the time of Hoffmann's first visit in 1947. Only twenty-five years earlier the local agricultural lobby had put forward a serious proposal for draining the entire Vaccarès. The bid, as we saw in Chapter 1, was only thwarted by the efforts of a more powerful lobby, the Société Nationale d'Acclimatisation de France, which had been formed in Paris during the previous century by a group of naturalists, scientists and powerful landowners dedicated—unfashionably at that time—to protect special areas of French countryside from urban and in-dustrial sprawl.

None the less, in spite of that narrow success, the threat of agri-cultural expansion was never likely to go away, especially with irrigation systems from the Rhône growing ever more sophisticated. Here, after all, was a constant supply of fresh water readily and cheaply available. When the Camargue Reserve was formed in 1929 it was seen as a welcome, although fragile, buffer between the salt companies on one side and the farming landowners on the other. It was in the interests of the former that the Vaccarès and the smaller lagoons in the area be maintained, as they put it, "in their natural and wild state". Wildlife was to be protected by courtesy of commerce. The Second World War produced fresh hazards. With an invasion by American and British troops imminent the German army proceeded to mine the Vaccarès as well as all adjacent lagoons that lay close to the sea. Removing the mines was to become a dangerous and laborious task. Then, in the early post-war a bullish French government, reasserting itself after the humiliations of the war, threatened to take over large areas of the Camargue for use as a military base.

Such was the uncertain background when the young Luc Hoffmann first arrived in the Camargue. It was as if the whole area had survived by the skin of its teeth. Hoffmann duly set to work. The Camargue, in his words, was "the biggest untouched area in France outside certain mountain districts, and biologically the richest in Europe." The Station Biologique, which he set up in 1954, became the first step towards the creation of a benevolent empire which has continued to expand ever since as a "hands on" research centre at the Tour du Valat. Hoffmann himself soon became an increasing influential figure internationally. In 1961 he helped establish the World Wildlife Fund, and became its vice-president. The Tour du Valat in turn benefited from its founder's fame and influence, and in 1971 the Fund made the foundation a gift of five million francs, enabling it to purchase further land immediately to the south of the existing property, known as the Petit Badon, swelling the foundation's' territory to a formidable six thousand acres.

Today the Tour du Valat looks as modest and unassuming as its distinguished founder. The turning off the by-road heading westwards towards the Grand Rhône is not even signposted, and the passing traveller would hardly know it was there. Like all engine-rooms, this one is well-hidden. Some of the most dense woodlands in the Camargue conceal what still gives the appearance of being the traditional *domaine* it once was—except for the number of cars scattered around the central courtyard brought here by a constant migration of visiting ecologists,

Ph.D students, professors and scientific advisers from Oxford, Cambridge, Nantes, Rennes, Montpellier, Groningen, Utrecht, Cairo and a host of other universities and institutions worldwide. Only a handsome new library building contradicts the dusty image of the place, its ranks of shelves bearing witness to the weight of the foundation's achievements. They are worthy of a university—which effectively the Tour du Valat is.

The optimistic message of the Tour du Valat is that a balance of interests in the Camargue is certainly possible—indeed it is essential if the region is to survive. In Dr. Hoffmann's words, "There is no incompatibility at all between nature conversation and development… The point at issue lies in management for biodiversity which must go hand in hand with the inevitable development of human activities."

Recent events described earlier in this chapter demonstrate how insecure that handshake can be. In the year 2007 the victim of that failure of collaboration was the Camargue's very emblem, the scarlet flamingo, which made the crisis especially poignant. At the time it was like the sinking of a flagship: if the flamingos should leave for good, what would be left of the Camargue? Accordingly it seems appropriate that the final chapter of this book should be devoted to the wildlife of this region, and in particular to the true royalty who reign here in the shape of that gawky, improbable-looking, ungainly beautiful creature that visitors come to see probably more than anything else—more even than the black bulls and the white horses, or the gypsies and the procession to the sea of Sara and the Two Marys: the Camargue flamingo.

Chapter Eleven

A BIRD'S-EYE VIEW

"No other large bird is so brightly coloured, and no other brightly coloured bird is so large." So wrote one of America's most distinguished ornithologists, Dr. Frank Chapman, in the early years of the twentieth century. The bird he was referring to was the Camargue flamingo, more correctly known as the Greater Flamingo, or more scientifically as *Phoenicopterus ruber*, the "red winged creature from Phoenicia", first so named by the Latin poet Juvenal in the first century AD.

But why Phoenicia? Possibly because the flamingos migrated each winter southwards to North Africa and the Middle East, where the Phoenicians had numerous outposts and colonies, in particular the commercial capital of their empire, Carthage. Alternatively, *Phoenicopterus* and Phoenicia may simply derive from the same Greek word for blood-red, *phoino*, since the Phoenicians liked to dress in that colour. Or yet again, it may have been merely a case of travellers' tales, the Phoenicians having for so many centuries been the great traders and navigators of the Mediterranean and beyond. So, it became known as the Phoenician bird, a creature seen to come and go with the seasons, forever on the move, like the Phoenician merchants. Like so many migratory birds, the flamingo has attracted legends.

Its breeding grounds have shrunk since Roman times, or been severely reduced in number, due of course to a vast increase in human population throughout the Mediterranean region, accompanied by the inevitable draining of marshlands and the expansion of agriculture. The invention of the shot-gun has done little to help it either. The flamingo, it is claimed, also dislikes disturbance, a trait scarcely compatible with western civilization in the twenty-first century, especially since the birds' preferred breeding-grounds are saltwater lagoons close to the sea, and therefore close to beaches frequented by holiday-makers.

The Camargue remains one of the very few places in the Mediterranean region where the Greater Flamingo has managed successfully to breed over the past centuries. There have been years (most recently 2007), as well as whole blocks of time, when the birds have failed to breed for a variety of reasons (to be touched on later); yet more often than not in recent decades between 30,000 and 40,000 *flamands roses*, as they are known in France, have nested here each year, producing two-thirds of the young birds hatched throughout the entire Mediterranean area. Much of the fame of the Camargue, as well as its special ecological importance, rests on this fact. That distinguished English naturalist, G. K. Yeates, described the huge colony of nesting flamingos in the Camargue as "the greatest spectacle in all the world of birds".

For a great many visitors the Camargue means, above all, birds. The place is a bird-watcher's paradise. It is claimed on reliable authority that no fewer than 330 species frequent the Camargue; and any number of guide-books are available to explain precisely what these birds are and where to find them. Yet anyone with long memories of the Camargue will find that an up-to-date check-list includes a number of unfamiliar species: birds which are either newly resident or else have only recently come to breed regularly. These newcomers include two species of heron. One is that handsome sentinel of the marshes, the

Great White Heron, which used to be a rare visitor from Central Europe until the mid-1960s, then began to turn up regularly, and since the mid-1990s has bred annually in small numbers. Then there is its more gregarious cousin, the white Cattle Egret, with its distinctive buff-coloured crown, which first arrived from Spain to breed in 1967, and now has an estimated breeding population of up to six thousand. Climate change may be partly responsible, but certainly the birds have added character to the area. In the process of their take-over Cattle Egrets have become among the most photographed creatures in the Camargue on account of their habit of perching on the backs of grazing horses, doing their hosts a welcome service by gobbling up the insects that feed on the horses' flesh.

These two recent immigrants have joined the long-term resident population of herons, the most conspicuous being the snow-white Little Egret, which is visible on just about every pool and stretch of water throughout the Camargue, creating familiar spots of white dotted across the wetlands. The egrets are often accompanied at a discreet distance by the larger Grey Heron (a bird familiar throughout Europe including, of course, Britain) and by the rather more timid Purple Heron. Other resident members of the heron family are shier still: the Night Heron, the Squacco Heron and the virtually invisible Great Bittern whose presence is often detectible only by its mournful booming call like a distant fog-horn.

No visitor to the Camargue in winter can remain unaware for long of two of its distinctive features. One is the enormous population of over-wintering duck which have flown south from Russia, Siberia and northern Scandinavia. The great majority of them are those miniature creatures, teal, the males displaying their elegant green stripe behind the eye and a distinctive splash of pale gold below the tail. Teal are among the most delightful of ducks with their busy get-on-with-it manner and their high-pitched whistling cry as if alerting the whole world to their arrival. They are said to number up to 50,000 in the marshes, though that count might be considerably reduced by the time the teal head north in early spring as a result of the second distinctive feature of the Camargue winter, the sound of a shot-gun. It is at this season more than any other when we are reminded that large tracts of the Rhône delta are privately owned and are used by local farmers and landowners primarily as hunting-grounds—which the entire area once was.

But if hunting in the Camargue is now controlled, other hazards to wildlife have emerged in more recent times. Added to the threats of pollution, aircraft noise and vastly increased numbers of tourists is the two-sided effect of modern agriculture, particularly rice-growing and the consequent loss of wild and uncultivated areas of land. Adaptable birds like egrets and herons have prospered from the paddy-fields and from the spread of agriculture in general, but less adaptable species have not; and these have tended to be the rarer species: the Pratincole, the gorgeously-coloured Roller and Bee-eater, the Red-legged Partridge and that most handsome of watchful predators, the Great Grey Shrike.

The Camargue remains, all the same, "the ornithologist's El Dorado", as G. K. Yeates described it. It was Yeates, too, who claimed to have been all but deafened by the sound of nightingales, which "seemed to be singing from every bush." The poet Roy Campbell, who lived in the region for some years, waxed lyrically in his autobiography on the same theme: "On a calm night the breeze used to bring the united voices of a thousand nightingales in full song, mixed with the scent of pine, thyme, rosemary and wild lavender."

Everyone who loves birds will have a shortlist of special favourites which the Camargue can satisfy. Serious bird-watchers often retain something of the hunter about them—the hunter with binoculars rather than the gun. Gazing at a display of birds out of the car window is not their style: it is far too easy. Birds need to be tracked down, stalked, waited for with infinite patience, preferably in inclement weather. They may even love the mistral as much as Dumas hated it. Hence secretive birds can be high on that shortlist of favourites. There is the magic of the Golden Oriole, only occasionally seen dipping between poplar trees, but more often detected by its distinctive fluting call. The Hoopoe, too, may be heard more easily than seen, with its "oop-oop-oop" call which gives the bird its name. There are even passionate ornithologists who will spend furtive hours waiting for a glimpse of the most secretive of all little brown birds, the Cetti's Warbler, its invisible presence advertised only by a grating "tick-a-tick-a-tick-a-tick" like a malfunctioning road-drill, a sound known to drive the wives of passionate bird-watchers to seek the solace of the nearest wine-bar and perhaps the divorce court.

Then there are the brightly-clad players who strut on the open stage of the lagoons. On the shallow waters of the *salins* and the freshwater pools, besides the ubiquitous herons and egrets, are the long-legged Avocets, Spoonbills and Black-winged Stilts, along with the occasional Glossy Ibis—a quartet of remarkably-shaped bills, all of them adapted in their different ways to extracting the required food from beneath the surface of the water. And overhead, providing aerial accompaniment to the wading birds, are the terns, graceful sea swallows of the wetlands, several varieties of them; while patrolling low over the reed-beds that dark hunter, the Marsh Harrier, is rarely far away.

The Camargue is a region of extraordinarily diverse terrain, and this diversity is matched by the variety of wildlife and plant-life which it sustains. One can picture it as a broad triangle with its base in the sea. This coastal strip of some fifty miles in length is composed of a barrier of dunes constantly battered and threatened by the sea, but for the most part bound by tough grasses, and sporting equally tough sea holly and sea spurge, and in the warmer months that beautiful plant which appears so unexpectedly in this bleached environment, the sand lily.

Within the protective barrier of dunes lie the lagoons, occupying almost one quarter of the total area of the Camargue. Included among them are two extensive areas of salt-pans, one of them close to Salin-de-Giraud in the east of the delta, the other near Aigues-Mortes further to the west (as described in Chapter 5). These salt-pans or *salins*, kept deliberately at a shallow level, are for this reason rich in wildlife feeding there, particularly wading birds, flamingos among them. On the other hand, due to the high concentration of salt, plant-life is all but non-existent. Within the lagoons lying inland of the sea-dyke and hence not given over to salt-production conditions are very different. Here salt-and fresh-water blend, a principal source being fresh-water drained from the rice-fields further inland still, or pumped in directly from the Rhône. The vegetation in these wetland areas is richly varied. Near the southern edge of the Vaccarès lagoon is a string of small wooded islands called collectively the Bois des Rièges. There are seven of them, and they are inaccessible except on horseback, wading there from the sea-dyke, or else from the Etang du Fournelet a little to the east. From either direction access is strictly forbidden without a permit, one reason among many being that the islands are home to the Camargue's wild boar, who take less than kindly to tourists.

The Bois are in origin ancient dunes, which are survivors of an earlier coastline many millennia ago. Over such a span of time silt piled up sufficiently to support a variety of plant-life including the tall white asphodel, clumps of white cistus, the yellow everlasting flower as well as the ubiquitous red poppy. But the most remarkable botanical specimen to be found on these small islands is the Phoenician Juniper—another link with Phoenicia! How these trees arrived here nobody knows for certain, but none the less this is the only place in Europe where they grow in the wild, and some of the trees have reached a height of over sixty feet and are calculated to be as much as four hundred years old.

History and legend blend indistinguishably in this area. The nearby Vaccarès, though not especially deep overall, is locally reputed to conceal a hole into which people have been known to disappear. Needless to say scientific evidence is lacking, yet the legend of the fearful hole is supported by the tale of sixteen German soldiers who set out on horseback to hunt wild boar on the Bois des Rièges during the Second World War, only to vanish without trace before even reaching the islands. There might seem to be a more likely explanation for enemy soldiers disappearing during a wartime occupation, yet the story fits the legend well.

The most popular tale of the Bois relates to an ageless Caliban-like creature said to have once taken refuge at this spot, known as *La Bèstio dóu Vaccarés* or *La Bête du Vaccarès* (the Beast of the Vaccarès). The beast

achieved celebrity status in France during the 1920s on the strength of
a romantic novel purporting to be a truthful account of this humanoid
figure, which had been encountered on these islands during the fifteenth century in a state of mournful solitude. The book suited the
mood of persecution and alienation that was cultivated by Provençal
writers between the wars, and it is no surprise that its author was a
member of the Félibrige circle of Provençal writers and the son-in law
of Marquis Baroncelli. He was Joseph d'Arbaud, who abandoned a
career as a lawyer to live deep in the Camargue in order, he explained,
to listen to the song of the earth and to be close to the genuine
Provençal people who had preserved their language and their traditions.

The seven islands which make up the Bois, as well as a host of
smaller islets scattered around them, each bear the name *radeau*,
meaning literally "raft", as though they were actually floating, which in
this landscape of reflections and mirages they often appear to be. All
outcrops of land rising above the surface of these lagoons have a look
of impermanence about them. These small islets, which are sometimes
submerged and sometimes dry out altogether, bear a different name on
the map: *sansouires* (the local word for "salt-marsh"). The *sansouires* are
by no means confined to tiny islands; they are the typical landscape of
the lower Camargue, made up of caked mud-flats streaked here and
there with dried salt, over which one can wander for hours keeping a
mental compass-bearing on a distant lighthouse or the church bell-
tower at Les Saintes-Maries. The Camargue white horses often graze
here, as well as—in the winter months—flocks of sheep which, as the
temperature soars, will be driven inland to richer pastures.

Being dried-out salt-marsh the vegetation in the *sansouires* is sparse,
but distinctive, and in the case of the sea holly extremely prickly. Mauve
sea lavender abounds, as do glasswort, seablite and sea purslane, along
with several varieties of *Salicornia*, or samphire, sometimes resembling
a rich harvest of pipe-cleaners. Perhaps the most attractive feature of
sansouire plant-life is the presence everywhere on the sandy edge of the
marsh of tamarisk bushes with their leaves as light as gossamer and
plumes of tiny pink flowers looking as is they have been sprayed on

with a powder-puff. (A warning is due here: wise locals will explain darkly that it is when the tamarisk is in bloom that most voracious of the Camargue's insects are on the hunt, the minute insignificant-looking *arabie*, there being some malign symbiosis between insect and flowering tree.)

Dividing the marshlands and lagoons of the middle and lower Camargue from the agricultural areas further inland are the extensive reed-beds, home to quantities of the region's bird-life, as well as to herds of the semi-wild white horses. In springtime the young green shoots of the phragmite reed, which predominates here, are a vital food plant for the horses, providing them with much of the sustenance they need after the long winter.

Inland from the dense reed-beds the Camargue opens out into farming country. For many centuries fear of marsh fever deterred farmers from expanding their activities in these low-lying areas, and traditionally the grazing-land has been used primarily for sheep over-wintering in huge numbers, as many as 80,000 in the region as a whole. The early-summer migration of sheep to mountain pastures, the transhumance, still takes place though on a smaller scale, so much former grazing-land now being under cultivation. For a stirring and romantic account of that sheep migration in former days, the curious-minded should dip into Frédéric Mistral's epic poem *Mirèio*, or *Mireille*.

A very different kind of romance is attached to the Camargue vineyards. In origin these almost certainly date back to Roman times; the Benedictine and Cistercian monks who established their "salt abbeys" here are also known to have planted vines on their low-lying estates. Though the production of wine has never been on the scale (or of the quality) of the Rhône valley or Languedoc, the Camargue vineyards have nevertheless earned a special footnote in the history of French viticulture. During the 1860s and 1870s a genus of plant lice native to the United States was introduced accidentally into Europe where it took a special liking to the local vines, before long destroying vast quantities of vineyards throughout the continent and dragging many of their owners into bankruptcy. The rogue insect was called *Phylloxera vitifo-*

liae. Eventually vines brought from across the Atlantic, which were resistant to the fatal louse, enabled the European grape industry to recover. In the meantime, though, certain areas had escaped the pestilence, one of them being the Camargue. The reason was the surprising effect of local weather conditions. The entire region being a flood-plain, the Camargue vineyards were frequently waterlogged for lengthy periods. The vines themselves had been accustomed to such drownings for many centuries, and had learnt to survive. The *Phylloxera* louse could not. Submersion had proved an effective, if accidental, cure for the worst disease ever to have struck the European grape industry.

More recently another industry requiring fields to be waterlogged for long periods has taken hold in the Camargue: rice growing. Rice had been cultivated here in small quantities during the nineteenth century following the new embankments of the Rhône, but only once a system of pumps had been established for controlling freshwater irrigation from the river did the Camargue become a candidate for the cultivation of rice on a large scale—comparable to areas of the Lombardy plain in Northern Italy, which traditionally had supplied much of that country's considerable demand. And after the Second World War it was rice from Italy that was brought in to be planted in the Rhône delta. The industry expanded throughout the 1950s, the chief effect on the landscape being to turn grazing-land into paddy-fields. Sheep, which had long been the primary resource for Camargue farmers, became increasingly squeezed out. Rice proved more profitable: besides, it did not require a laborious trek to the mountains and back every year. It was not only the rice-farmers who profited from rice-growing. Wading birds, herons and egrets in particular, found the shallow paddy-fields much more to their liking than dry sheep meadows. The new partnership worked well until the birds soon developed a taste for the delicacy of young rice shoots, so invoking the punitive wrath of the rice-farmers who turned out with their shot-guns, to the consequent outrage of the bird-lovers. It became yet another diplomatic balancing act between wildlife and commerce, of a kind which those living and working in the Camargue were by now all too well accustomed.

To these principal geographical areas—the dunes, the *salins*, the wooded islands, the lagoons, the *sansouires*, the reed-beds, the vineyards, the grazing-land and the rice-fields—should be added two more: the forests, and the Crau. The Camargue forests are scarce and scattered. In former times they were dense and covered much of the freshwater area of the delta; the ships Julius Caesar commissioned from Arles, we have seen, may well have been built of locally cut hardwood timber. But agriculture has made giant inroads, and today the forests survive in patches or in strips—the patches being by and large where the minor branches of the Rhône used to flow, the strips being the thickly-wooded verges of today's Rhône, both the Petit and in particular the Grand Rhône.

To the east of the Grand Rhône lies that stretch of marshland and lagoon known as the Grand Plan du Bourg. Further east still, beyond the reach of river water, is that parched and mysterious region described in Chapter 1 and known as the Crau. It is not strictly speaking part of the Camargue at all, yet it is so close, and so dramatically different, that it asks to be included in any bird's-eye view of the region. If Provence can claim to have a desert, it is here. It is a sea of stones, in origin the dried river-bed of the Durance, which now flows elsewhere, joining the Rhône further north. Traditionally it is the land of sheep, which somehow manage to find something on which to graze among the prickly bushes that grow apparently out of the stones themselves. The sheep have always wintered here, joining their Camargue counterparts in early summer on the great migration to the mountains, the transhumance.

The bleakness of the Crau has always had its admirers, bird-watchers in particular, much of the wildlife being quite distinct from that of the Camargue itself. Being flat and largely open, there is little concealment for the local birds, though the Pin-tailed Sand Grouse, the Stone Curlew and the Little Bustard are adept at disguising themselves as just another pile of stones. But that openness is also an invitation to another local "resident", the mistral. Few writers visiting the Crau have failed to respond to its ferocity. Alexandre Dumas, drawn by his romantic spirit to the legendary site of Hercules' Eleventh Labour, was caught by so powerful a mistral that he swore it was capable of carrying off an entire flock of sheep. The ornithologist G. K. Yeates, who attempted to set up hides in order to photograph birds in the region, claimed with exasperation that the mistral "takes the skin off your nose like a banana." Even Vincent Van Gogh, who ventured only to the northerly fringe of the Crau when he set up his easel by the roadside to paint his celebrated *Harvest* with the blue Alpilles hills in the background, was moved to confide to his brother Theo: "When the mistral blows it is precisely the opposite here of a gentle land, for the mistral is an irritation. And yet what revenge, what revenge," he added, "when there is a day without a wind. What intensity of colour, what pure air."

One wishes Van Gogh could have remained longer in this region, or had been able to venture more frequently into the depths of the delta. How many masterpieces did his row with Gauguin and subsequent departure from Provence deprive us of, one wonders. As it is, his few dazzling paintings and drawings of the Camargue and the surrounding area still stand as the most eloquent witnesses we have of its haunting and elusive beauty.

A final salute must be given in honour of the true royalty of the Camargue, namely the Scarlet Flamingo, the *flamand rose*, with which this chapter opened. So, what do we know about them in relation to the Camargue? They have probably bred here since time immemorial, though the earliest reliable record is from the late eighteenth century when a French naturalist by the name of Darluc mentioned the fact in his *Histoire Naturelle de Provence*. A hundred years later, in the 1880s, one of the first writers to record the various breeding colonies of flamingos in Europe was a remarkable English sportsman, Abel Chapman (no relation to his American namesake quoted at the beginning of this chapter). In a manner characteristic of so many adventurous Victorian travellers, Chapman combined the role of keen naturalist and conservationist with a passion for slaughtering vast numbers of creatures wherever he travelled. Chapman's principal association with the flamingo was in southern Spain where he became a manager of a forty-mile stretch of coastal marshland, the Coto Doñana, which he proceeded to run as a nature reserve—an enterprise at least a century ahead of its time. Here he identified, and recorded, the major breeding-ground in Europe of the Greater Flamingo. In the course of studying the migratory and breeding habits of the bird he extended his researches to the Camargue, putting the region firmly on the map as a second regular breeding-ground of the bird.

Since then a number of naturalists have made detailed studies of the flamingo in the Camargue. One of the earliest checklists was drawn by an Englishman, W. E. Glegg, in 1931. A Frenchman, L. Gallet, followed in 1949. At much the same time the young Swiss biologist, Luc Hoffmann, made a study of flamingos the first scientific project to be undertaken under the auspices of the biological station he was in the process of establishing at the Tour du Valat.

As a result of these and numerous other studies a great deal was learnt about the birds, their needs and their habits. It was established that their food consisted of small invertebrates—protozoa, algae, crustaceans, molluscs, worms—all consumed by means of a filtering system consisting of plates covered in hairs on the inside of their bills. It was also established that the reddish coloration of their feathers was due to the "carotene" content of their food, which became metabolized into pigments distributed throughout the birds' bodies.

It became clear, too, that the breeding pattern of Camargue flamingos was alarmingly fragile, and has been so for a long time. As recently as the 1930s there was only a small nesting colony. Unaccountably numbers then increased. During the Second World War it was recorded that as many as 2,000 pairs succeeded in nesting, after which numbers continued to grow for more than a decade until, quite unexpectedly, in 1962 the nesting birds produced no young at all; two years later they ceased to nest altogether. The finger of blame pointed in several directions. Pollution from agricultural fertilizers and from huge industrial expansion to the east of the Grand Rhône. Low-flying training aircraft operating from the military airfield on the southern edge of the Crau. General disturbance caused by increased tourism. Inadequate water levels. The wrong kind of water. Shortage of the right food. And so on. Local communists blamed the French government. The government authorities blamed just about everybody else. There were even stern local voices claiming the disaster to be a punishment inflicted by the three Marys for the growing commercialization of the Camargue.

Then inexplicably, and to the vast relief of naturalists and holiday-makers alike, in 1969 the flamingos returned to breed, not just in one site but two, one of them being the Etang du Fangassier. This heartening event seems to have been the trigger for the scientists to move in. The first priority was to take measures to ensure that the long hiatus in breeding, which had lasted seven years, would not recur. The authorities at the Tour du Valat, led by Dr. Hoffmann, took the initiative. Putting into practice the knowledge they had acquired of the birds' nesting requirements, they mounted an experiment. They persuaded the local salt company, the Compagnie des Salins du Midi, who owned the lagoon where the flamingos had returned to breed, to build an island 720 feet long and a little over one and a half feet high in the Etang du Fangassier, large enough to accommodate at least 800 pairs of birds, so it was estimated.

Construction work was made possible by the drying out of large areas of the lagoon during the winter months. At first the experiment seemed to have failed; the flamingos took no notice of their new accommodation for three years. Finally, in 1973, at an international symposium held at the Wildfowl Trust in Slimbridge, Gloucestershire, under the auspices of Sir Peter Scott, the idea was floated that the flamingos might appreciate further help in order to breed. The trouble with the man-made island, it was suggested, was that it was only an island; in order to attract the birds it might need to be made to look like an existing nesting site. Flamingos were known to nest on raised hillocks. Accordingly it was proposed that a veritable "housing estate" of artificial mounds, made of local mud, be constructed on the island. The proposal was accepted by the Tour du Valat authorities and by the salt company.

The following winter visitors to the eastern Camargue were puzzled to witness a team of volunteers in tall boots transporting buckets of mud from the lagoon and modelling it into what resembled large up-turned flowerpots right across the island—five hundred of them to begin with, and soon as many more.

Three months later, in the summer of 1974, over one thousand pairs of flamingos successfully bred there. Accommodation was cramped, and in limited supply, but it was enough. And over the decades to follow the number of birds nesting here rose to an estimated 35,000. A new era for the flamingo city had begun.

It was an era that lasted thirty-two years—until the events of 2007, described in the previous chapter, brought it to a temporary end. Whether another new era for the flamingos has begun is still unclear. We can only wait, and hope.

The magic of the Camargue is elusive. It is a region of reflections and mirages, with so much that is fleeting, and so much that is vivid and varied. It is a place of history. At its borders stand those noble gateways, Arles and St. Gilles, behind which rise imperious ghosts: Julius Caesar, the Emperor Constantine, the militant popes, the rebel counts of Toulouse, the doomed Cathars. Then there are the faithful pilgrims who gathered in the abbey church before departing on foot for Spain and Santiago de Compostela, and the great bastion of Aigues-Mortes with its echoes of the French king St. Louis and the two crusades he led to the Holy Land. Echoes, too, of the heroic Protestant women imprisoned there for ever for their stubborn faith. And the craggy fortified church of Les Saintes-Maries-de-la-Mer built to receive the legend and the bones of the Marys and the gypsy queen Sara. Finally the vanished salt abbeys and the *commanderies* of the Knights of St. John, whose only legacy is the range of salt mountains lining the Mediterranean shore.

These mirages of history form the backdrop to the living Camargue

of today—a wilderness of marsh, lake and salt-water, the very essence of the place, with its black bulls, its wild horses, its lagoons and broad skies, and of course its wildlife all around.

The evening is the perfect time to savour the magic of the Camargue. This is the moment when the last of the sunlight seems to acquire a dark filter, sharpening the colours of the marshes and the vast lagoons. Across the sheets of water flamingos are dotted in their thousands like brushstrokes of scarlet paint, their long necks lowered as their curved beaks scoop for food beneath the surface. Suddenly for some invisible reason the birds begin to grow restless, raising their heads questioningly until all of a sudden they take off as if obeying an unheard signal. This is what in French is called their *envol*. Then the fly-past begins. From across the lagoons the flamingos gather into a loose formation, only to turn together against the setting sun before passing silently overhead like a string of jewels in the sky. The monarchs of the Camargue have put on their evening show.

Further Reading

Adshead, S. A. M., *Salt and Civilisation*. (Basingstoke, 1992)

Aldington, R., *Introduction to Mistral*. (London, 1956)

Ali, S.A., *A Short History of the Saracens*. (London, 1949)

Barber, M., *The Cathars: Dualist Heretics in Languedoc in the High Middle Ages*. (London, 2000)

Barenger, R., *En Camargue avec Baroncelli*. (Nîmes, 1992)

Baroncelli-Javon, le Marquis F. de, *Blad de Luno*. (Avignon, 1909)

_____, *L'Elevage en Camargue de taureaux*. (Drôme, 1931)

Benoît, F., *La Camargue*. (Paris, 1933)

Blondel J. and Isenman P., *Guide des oiseaux de Camargue*. (Paris, 1981)

Campbell, R., *Sons of the Mistral*. (London, 1941)

_____, *Light on a Dark Horse: an Autobiography*, 1901-1935. (London, 1951)

Chapman, F. M., *Camps and Cruises of an Ornithologist*. (London, 1908)

Clébert, J-P., *The Gypsies*. (London, 1963)

Cook. T. A., *Old Provence*. (Oxford, 2001)

d'Arbaud, J., *La Bête du Vaccarès*. (Paris, 1926)

d'Elly, R., *La Camargue gardiane* (Paris, 1938 and 1944)

Daudet, A., *Lettres de mon moulin*. (Paris, 1910)

Delpech, J., and Vartabedian, S., *Images of the Camargue* (Blois, 2002)

Dix, C., *The Camargue*. (London, 1975)

Droit, M., *Camargue*. (London, 1963)

Dumas, A., *From Paris to Cadiz* . (London, 1958)

_____, *Pictures of Travel in the South of France*. (London, 1951)

Duncan, P., *Horses and Grasses*. (New York, 1992)

Durrell, L., *Caesar's Vast Ghost: Aspects of Provence*. (London, 1990)

_____, *Spirit of Place: Letters and Essays on Travel* (London, 1969)

Flandrey, J. de, *Folco de Baroncelli*. (Avignon, 1947)

Fraser, A., *The Gypsies*. (Oxford, 1992)

Garrett, M., *Provence: a Cultural History*. (Oxford, 2006)

Giono, J., *Camargue*. (Lausanne, 1960)

Glegg, W. E., *The Birds of L'Ile de Camargue et Petit Camargue*. (London, 1931)

Gueusque, M.-F., *La Provence arlésienne: traditions et avatars*. (Arles, 2000)

Guyonnet, M.-H., *L'Empire du sel* (Musée Camarguais, c. 2006)

Hemingway, E., *The Garden of Eden*. (London, 1987)

Isenman, P. (ed.), *Les Oiseux de Camargue et leurs habitats: une histoire de cinquante ans 1954-2004*. (Paris, 2004)

_____, *Birds of the Camargue*. (Clichy, 1993)

James, H., *A Little Tour in France*. (London, 1987)

John, A., *Autobiography*. (London, 1975)

_____, *Chiaroscuro* (London, 1952)

Johnson, A., *Les Flamands de Camargue*. (Parc de Camargue 1992)

Joinville, J. de, *Life of St. Louis*. (London, 1955)

Jolivet, D., *La Camargue au Coeur*. (Montpellier, 1991)

Jouveau, R., *Histoire du Félibrige*. (Nîmes, 1970)

Kasson, J., *Buffalo Bill's Wild West: Celebrity, Memory and Popular History*. (New York, 2000)

Krippner, M., *Discovering the Camargue*. (London, 1960)

Kunansky, M., *Salt: a World History*. (London, 2002)

Labarge, M. W., *Saint Louis: the Life of Louis IX of France*. (London, 1968)

Lambert, M. D., *The Cathars*. (Oxford, 1998)

Le Goff, L., *Saint Louis*. (Paris, c.1996)

Lékai, L., *The White Monks: a History of the Cistercian Order*. (Wisconsin, 1953)

Madaule, J., *The Albigensian Crusade*. (London, 1967)

Martin, S., *The Cathars*. (Harpenden, 2005)

Mistral, F., *Mireille*. (Avignon, 1867)

_____, *Mes Origines*. (London, 1907)

Molina, J., *Flore de Camargue*. (Parc de Camargue 1996)

Mullins, E., *The Pilgrimage to Santiago* (Oxford, 2001)

_____, *In Search of Cluny: God's Lost Empire*. (Oxford, 2006)

_____, *Avignon of the Popes, City of Exiles*. (Oxford, 2007)

O'Shea, S., *The Perfect Heresy: the Life and Death of the Cathars*. (London, 2000)

Rice, M., *The Power of the Bull*. (London, 1998)

Richard, J., *Saint Louis: Crusader King of France*. (Cambridge, 1992)

Roche, A. V., *Provençal Regionalism*. (Illinois, 1954)

Schama, S., *Landscape and Memory*. (London, 1995)

Stendhal (Beyle, M. H.), *Travels in the South of France*. (London 1971)

Sumption, J., *The Albigensian Crusade*. (London, 1978)

Sylvester, H., and Delavoiue S., *Horses of the Camargue*. (New York, 2002)

Tobin, S., *The Cistercians: Monks and Monasteries of Europe*. (London, 1995)

Van Gogh, V., *The Letters of Van Gogh* (ed. Roskill, R.). (London, 1983)

Vlassis, G., *Oiseaux en Camargue*. (Aix-en-Provence, 1990)

Weber, K., and Hoffmann, L., *Camargue: the Soul of a Wilderness*. (London, 1968)

Yeates, G. K., *Bird Life of Two Deltas*. (London, 1946)

_____, *Flamingo City*. (London, 1950)

Zaretsky, R., *Cock and Bull Stories, Folco de Baroncelli and the Invention of the Camargue*. (Nebraska 2004)

USEFUL WEBSITES

- www.camargue.fr
  general Camargue portal
- www.beyond.fr/sites/camargue
  introduction to the region
- www.saintesmaries.com
  website of Les Saintes-Maries-de-la-Mer tourist office
- www.nacioun-gardiano.fr
  French-only website of Nacioun Gardiano

Index

Index

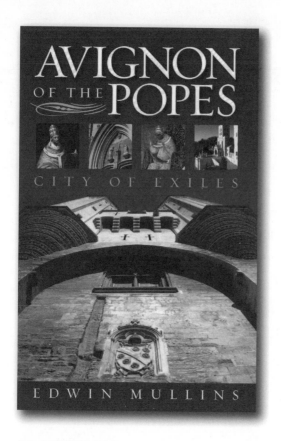

978-1-904955-56-6
2008, 256 pp, paperback, £9.99

Avignon of the Popes
CITY OF EXILES

At the beginning of the fourteenth century, anarchy in Italy led to the capital of the Christian world being moved from Rome—for the first and only time in history. It was a critical moment, and it resulted in seven successive popes remaining "in exile" for the next seventy years. The city chosen to replace Rome was Avignon. And depending on where you stood at the time they were seventy years of heaven, or of hell—opinions invariably ran to extremes, as did the behaviour of the popes themselves.

It was during this period of exile that the city witnessed some of the most turbulent events in the history of Christendom, among them the suppression of the Knights Templar and the last of the heretical Cathars, the first onslaught of the Black Death, the final collapse of the crusading dream, and the first decades of the Hundred Years War between England and France, in which successive Avignon popes attempted to mediate. The papal flight from Rome was fiercely castigated by Dante in *The Divine Comedy*, while during the later years of papal Avignon the enigmatic figure of Petrarch, the most celebrated poet and scholar of his day, loomed angrily over the city. In a dramatic *dénouement*, Avignon became home to the "antipopes", rivals and enemies of the re-established Roman papacy.

This is a portrait sketch of that era. And at the centre of the picture is Avignon itself, as it grew from being a relatively insignificant town on the Rhône to become, albeit briefly, one of the great capitals of the world.

> "Describes one of the most remarkable episodes in the history of the Middle Ages… This is history made thoroughly evocative and engaging." Ross King, author, *Brunelleschi's Dome*

> "An excellent introduction to a critical period in the history of medieval Europe and the church. Mullins provides a well-balanced and sympathetic treatment of popes often denigrated for their lack of piety." Michael Frassetto, author, *The Great Medieval Heretics*

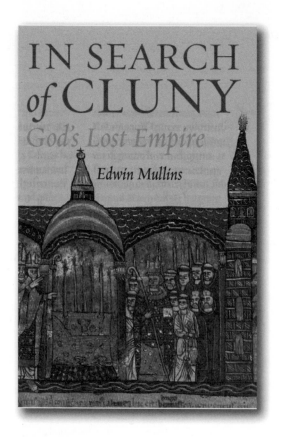

978-1-904955-04-7
2006, 256 pp, hardback, £16.99

In Search of Cluny
GOD'S LOST EMPIRE

A thousand years ago the French abbey of Cluny was the hub of one of the most powerful empires of the Middle Ages, and the spiritual heart of Europe. Nearly 1,500 religious houses were subject to its authority, and it was the seat of immense political power throughout the Christian world. The abbots of Cluny were among the most formidable men of their day; they were friends and advisers to successive popes and Holy Roman Emperors, as well as to the kings of England, France and Spain. They were also among the greatest builders the world has known, responsible for some of the finest mediaeval architecture, painting and sculpture.

This book tells the story of the abbey from its humble beginnings as a hunting-lodge given to a Benedictine monk by the local duke, through its centuries of glory, to its long decline until the French Revolutionary mob vandalized the buildings and it was auctioned to local entrepreneurs as a stone quarry. It also tells the story of the men involved in this vast enterprise, individuals of exceptional determination and single-mindedness, whose faith co-existed with extraordinary political acumen.

Reconstructing the lives, beliefs and ambitions of Cluny's abbots, Edwin Mullins puts the abbey and its network of dependent monasteries at the centre of medieval European history. He examines its vital contribution to the Reconquest of Spain from the Saracens, its role in organizing the First Crusade to the Holy Land and its conciliatory part in the violent struggles between popes and the Holy Roman Emperor. He also considers Cluny's relationship to England and William the Conqueror following the Norman Conquest of 1066 and the bitter conflict with St. Bernard of Clairvaux and rival Cistercian monasteries.

Much of Cluny's enduring legacy lies in the cultural innovations that the abbey sponsored, and *In Search of Cluny* traces the institution's influence on the great mediaeval pilgrimage to Santiago de Compostela, as well as its contribution to the magnificent carved churches of Moissac, Autun and Vézelay.

"A labour of love, dense with recondite information lovingly chronicled and written in a lucid, aphoristic style." *The Independent*

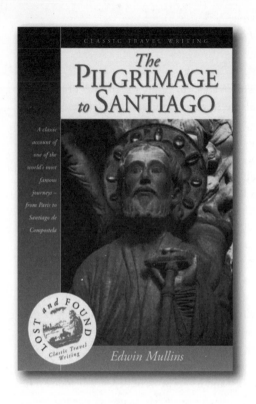

978-1-902669-31-2
2006 reprinted and corrected, 224pp, paperback, £9.99

The Pilgrimage to Santiago

"The Long Road to Heaven", the annual pilgrimage to the Galician city of Santiago de Compostela has taken place for over a thousand years. In the great cathedral of Santiago are said to lie the bones of St. James of the Great, cousin to Christ, an original disciple and later "resurrected" as the legendary slayer of the Moors. From the Middle Ages onwards, this most evocative of Christian shrines has attracted pilgrims to the Spanish city from all over Europe and further afield. A network of routes, lined with statues and other symbols, leads to Santiago, but the most celebrated is that from Paris, across the Pyrenees and through the arid uplands of northern Spain.

Following in their footsteps, Edwin Mullins takes the pilgrim route, fascinated by its extraordinary historical and religious symbolism. Journeying by car and by foot, he retraces the path from the Rue St. Jacques in Paris to the Baroque magnificence of Santiago's cathedral. On his way, he recounts the legends of Charlemagne, Roland and St. James himself, exploring the ideological dimension of the spiritual pilgrimage and the proliferation of religious orders around the route. He also looks at the pilgrims themselves, their motives and experiences, the millions of people "who walked the same journey out of love, out of punishment, duty, fear, or out of simple blind faith."

First published in 1974 and now reissued with a new Preface, this classic account of one of Europe's most stirring journeys provides an amalgam of history and geography, religion and archaeology, fact and legend. Illustrated with specially taken photographs, *The Pilgrimage to Santiago* is both a narrative account of the pilgrims' route and an analysis of a remarkably enduring religious phenomenon.

> "Mullins (is) a scholar and wordsmith par excellence… An astute work based on well-founded sources and the author's erudition. This superb panorama of art, religion, history and architecture will provide delightful reading." *Library Journal*